High Ambitions

High Ambitions

JAMIE ROONEY WITH PHIL HODGSON

VERTICAL EDITIONS

www.verticaleditions.com

First published in the United Kingdom
in 2009 by Vertical Editions,
Unit 4a, Snaygill Industrial Estate, Skipton,
North Yorkshire BD23 2QR

www.verticaleditions.com

ISBN 978-1-904091-29-5

A CIP catalogue record for this book is
available from the British Library.

Cover design and typeset by HBA, York

Printed and bound by the
MPG Books Group, Bodmin

CONTENTS

1

SHIFTING PRIORITIES

Professional rugby league players universally regarded The Boulevard, the former home of Hull FC, as a bear pit before the Airlie Birds moved to the KC Stadium. Because of this I wasn't particularly worried about feeling a little more nervous than usual as I set off to join the rest of the Wakefield Trinity Wildcats squad for the 60-mile coach trip along the M62. We were facing a tough game—no one ever expected anything else against a side that was always fiercely committed in front of their notoriously vociferous fans in the infamous Threepenny Stand—but we were reasonably confident that if we could perform at somewhere around our best we would return to West Yorkshire with a win under our belts.

But I didn't make it to Hull. In fact I didn't even get as far as our Belle Vue ground. Thoughts about anything as relatively insignificant as sport vanished when a call from Erika turned my world upside down. I've known and loved Erika for over a decade now. She's a strong, feisty character and not given to tears. In all that time I've rarely known her to cry. She was crying now, though. In fact she could hardly get her words out through the tears.

Her routine visit to the doctor with our baby son Brennan had brought shattering news which threw our lives into immediate turmoil and which would affect our family and friends for the rest of our days. 'Brennan has cerebral palsy,' she managed to blurt out. She repeated, as if she couldn't believe her own words, 'He's got cerebral palsy.'

I didn't really know, then, what cerebral palsy was—I do now—but I knew it was serious. And now it was my turn to cry. 'I'm coming straight home,' was all I could say. 'I'm coming back.'

I don't know to this day what I said when I rang Trinity coaches Shane McNally and Adrian Vowles, or what I blurted out to our captain Brad Davies. From what I learned later, I was almost unintelligible but clearly devastated. Being the decent blokes they are they didn't hesitate in giving me permission to turn back. And from that moment on rugby league, which had been the most important thing in my life for the best part of two decades and which remains part of my very soul, would have to share equal billing with my son and the rest of my family.

2

BIRTHDAY CELEBRATIONS

Erika is partial to her Strongbow, it's long been her favourite tipple, and she had more reason than usual to crack open a can or two of the popular cider on 9 October 2007. It wasn't just because of the fact that we were all gathered together to celebrate Brennan's fifth birthday. That was reason enough for a happy atmosphere, of course, as it would be in any family, and our own tribe were round in numbers to help us enjoy the occasion. What made it an extra-special day was without any doubt the best bit of news we'd had for a very long time. Increasingly concerned about Brennan's condition, and spinning round like tops amidst conflicting and confusing advice from the medics, we'd already determined on taking him over to Germany. We'd heard that a specialist in Ratingen near Dusseldorf could help him make real progress and, hopefully, with all our fingers and toes crossed, play a key role in improving his prospects for a better life.

We'd been told, though, that problems surrounding Brennan's hip, which was out of place, would have to be overcome before anything at all would be possible. I'm not sure if there's a God smiling down on us (Erika is also undecided). But we both edged closer to being believers in the Almighty when some fantastic news came through as we were helping an excited Bren open his cards and presents. His hip, incredibly, had gone back into place somehow. And we could now fly him to Germany for the treatment that we believed represented perhaps his last chance of leading, in his childhood, into his youth and throughout his adulthood, something like a normal life. It was almost unbelievable, particularly coming on such a special day, and it was a massive and positive boost for us all.

Our tentative plans, made almost more in hope than expectation, to take Brennan to Germany now suddenly became hard-and-fast reality, and our mood was as high as it's possible to get—in marked contrast to that day, on 27 June 2003 (I'm not good on dates but I'll never forget that one) when we found out about Brennan's condition. He suffers from a particularly virulent form of quadriplegic cerebral palsy, which affects both of his arms, each of his legs, and his trunk. His condition is what the medics tell us is termed the 'stiff' one. It causes him to have regular spasms and another aspect is that he has a high muscle tone, which makes it difficult for him to use any of his four limbs. In addition to being stiff in the arms and legs, the quadriplegic cerebral palsy condition causes sufferers to be unable to sit up unaided; they are invariably floppy in the trunk, and as if that isn't enough, they have the same difficulty in the neck. When Brennan was a baby he couldn't, try as he might, hold his head up. His fists were clenched, like a boxer's fists, his thumbs were turned in and he cried constantly, almost without a break it seemed, except while he was asleep, for the first nine months of his life.

Brennan, as it happens, was our first child, so we simply didn't know whether all this was normal or whether it was something to be concerned about. Anyone who has had kids will agree, I'm certain, that there are occasions when, whether we like to admit it as parents or not, we are not at all sure about things. Most parents, because of this, tend to err on the safe side and generally take their children to the doctor for the simplest thing. Most professionals understand this and mums and dads will, almost without fail, find that the medics are understanding, caring, attentive and helpful.

We've followed the same pathway with Fletcher, Brennan's younger brother, as a matter of course, taking him to the surgery for the slightest thing—simply because you can't be too careful. It's more as a precaution usually, but with Brennan we really did feel—although we struggled to put our fingers on it—that something was wrong. Erika and I kept taking him back to Pontefract Hospital and telling them that something obviously wasn't right. Unfortunately, our pleas generally fell on deaf ears. The doctors there insisted, time after time, that we were being paranoid because he was our first child, and that his screaming and his posture was merely because he'd been born prematurely. They maintained that it was nothing more than colic, and they kept sending us away. But Erika, as a mum, sensed that something wasn't quite right. Sadly, she was correct.

The whole issue seemed, from what they told us, to stem around the early birth. His birth ironically, began on the evening that I was away collecting an award as a member of the team of the year, with the rest of the Featherstone Rovers side, coaching staff, sponsors and board members, at the Northern Ford Premiership (NFP) Presentation Night at Elland Road, the home of the Leeds United soccer side.

Brennan wasn't due for another nine weeks, so there wasn't an issue in me toddling off to the bash. But Erika had, that morning, felt that something was imminent and went to see her GP about it. The doctor said it was just Braxton Hicks and nothing more but that night, after I'd gone to the NFP 'do', Erika knew she was in labour. By the time she got to Pontefract Hospital she was 7.5 centimetres dilated. That was, for us, definitely a factor in Brennan's condition.

Erika was given steroids when I got to the hospital, having dashed over from Leeds, but it was too late. Brennan cried immediately—which is of course normal for most births—and although he was given good scores when they filled in all their charts, they subsequently ventilated him for an hour after he was born, and we now understand that can be a cause of cerebral palsy. Erika frets about the ventilation. She really can't understand, try as she might, why they did it, and in truth neither can I. It seems, from what we can gather, that they were trying to help him breathe through a machine, but he was crying anyway, he had good colouring, and had been given good scores, so we do question, even now, whether it was necessary.

Brennan wouldn't settle. He couldn't sleep, he cried all the time, and all in all it was a very difficult period. We didn't have our own house at that time; Erika was at Jessica's (her sister's) and we were flitting between there, her mum's and my mum's, all the while trying to get some professional help, because Brennan was so bad. Erika, bless her, was pretty much at the end of her tether for six months. We had a lot of support, our families helped as much as they could and we'll always be very grateful for that, but it was a very tough period and it continued the same way pretty much until I got my contract with Wakefield in December 2002.

Everybody was fantastic, and our families couldn't have been more supportive and welcoming. But there's no getting away from the fact that you do feel uncomfortable in someone else's house, no matter who that person is or how close they may be to you. Erika will tell you if you ask her how Jessica often used to get up in the middle of the night with her and sit downstairs, trying together to comfort Brennan, and how it all felt so unreal. Nothing would calm him and they couldn't settle him no matter what they tried. He produced a constant, continual scream; not like a cry at all, more like a high-pitched scream, as if he was in pain all the time. That was the only way

Erika could describe it; and, of course, he **was** in pain, although we didn't know it then.

He was tight, wound up like a little ball. The doctor kept asking us whether he was pulling his knees up towards his chest and stomach—which he was—and advising us that it was colic. 'It's in his stomach,' she would say in answer to our increasingly anxious questions. 'Just try these drops to soothe him.' Which we did, repeatedly— but nothing quietened him down. Brennan wasn't interested in rattles or toys or any bits and pieces like that, which was something else that bothered us. We went back to the hospital about four weeks after we first found out he was poorly, and they did some tests and discovered that he was blind. He had been born blind, but we're glad to say that his eye muscles have developed since then. He's now visually impaired, but he can see; they've stimulated him with light systems, which has been a fantastic development. The improvement happened gradually, and it involved more than his sight. We started to notice that he was starting to follow things, and lift his arm up.

Later, after we'd been back many times and when Brennan's condition had become obvious, they repeatedly asked us whether Erika drank or smoked, delving into her habits. To us, rightly or wrongly, the impression was that they appeared to be attempting to shift the blame back on to us. They hadn't even picked up on his condition, the physiotherapist had noticed fairly quickly that Brennan cried all the time—you could hardly miss that, to be honest—and that he wanted to be handled constantly.

Anyway, they called us back for an appointment (this is when they knew the reality of the situation—Brennan was nine months old by this stage) which I couldn't attend because of Wakefield's game at Hull. That's when the truth was revealed to Erika. I wish to this day that I'd been with her at the time.

Brennan, the brave little lad, had it very tough in those traumatic early months and we're glad that he was too young to be able to remember it. The pain from the spasms was everywhere, throughout his body. Some kids just have spasms in their legs, others will have it limited to their arms, while still others suffer in their trunk, but our Brennan had it in every part of his body. His arms were tight to his chest, his legs were crossing, his hands were closed shut, and he was in pain all the time, with no relief whatsoever. They described it as being like constant cramps, all over his body. It still happens in the night, when he'll get it in his arms and his legs and it wakes him up.

They decided to put him on the drug Baclofen, which reduces muscle tone, to limit his cramps. We were told to give him a dose at night; after 12 hours it would have faded and there would be no lasting effects in the day. But he was just lethargic and not interested in anything, so we took him off it. Then they gave us a sleeping drug, Melatonin, but that didn't work either. In fact nothing has worked. We've tried everything we've been able to think of or uncover, we even took the drastic step of taking him to a sleep clinic for a year, to try to get some advice from a different source on how to get him settled best, but nothing we tried worked at all.

After all this, things were at last looking up with the news over Brennan's hip. It was great news for him and it was a fantastic development for all of us. We're a close family, and that's so important at times like this. I'm not saying that sport is the same—Brennan's experiences have given me a better sense of perspective than perhaps I used to have—but there are certainly comparisons which can justifiably be made. In sport, you need your family around you, because there are so many ups and downs. I think I've got one of the best in Erika and the kids, my mum, her mum and our brothers and sisters. We're a close family and I don't see how I could possibly be where I am today without them.

Obviously my family are a major part of my life but as a professional rugby league player I've also got to be fully focussed on my performance on the pitch. Every now and then I need a kick up the backside from Erika to get my act together and I have to say that she's very ready to give it! She's been watching rugby since she's been with me, for well over 12 years now, and it quickly became a big part of her life. She knows when I'm not playing well; she doesn't like to get involved too much but I've come to realise that when I'm due a rollicking she'll give me one. If I'm moping around the house after a bad game, for example, she'll tell me to stop feeling sorry for myself, that it isn't going to solve anything and brings me back down to earth.

Little things like that are so important. I'm sure if you ask any rugby league player, or any other sportsman, whether he be a soccer player, a cricketer, an athlete, a boxer or even something more esoteric like a chess player, that they'll all say much the same. One minute you're up, the next minute you're down. If you've lost, or if you've had a bad game, you're inevitably going to be fed up with yourself and you just won't be able to wait for the next week to put it right again. And if you play well? Well, you're on a high, and that can be just as wearing, I suppose, for those around you.

I think, when I try to stand outside myself and analyse myself dispassionately, that I tend to be one of those players who, if his team has lost, believes he hasn't played well and that he is at fault for the defeat. I know it's a team game and that some in the side will have performed better than others, win or lose, but it doesn't matter one iota what anyone will say to me about my own performance. For me, it's cut and dried. I haven't played well in my own eyes if we've been beaten. The team needs to win for me to believe that I've done okay—and that's despite the margin between victory and defeat in modern-day rugby league often being very narrow, so narrow in many cases as should almost make no difference.

I try not to take my game home with me, and the kids certainly help with that. Fletcher, who like Brennan was born prematurely—in his case by six weeks—also spent his early days in the special unit at Pontefract but he's doing fine now. I love them both dearly and if I can be half the father to my children that my own dad was to me, I think I'll have done very well for my kids. Brennan obviously won't play rugby but if Fletch wants to play—and the signs are that he will have plenty of ability—I'll support him to the hilt. Bren might turn out to be a little whiz kid or something like that, but for now he enjoys Fletcher running around the house. Erika and I are bringing our lads up to enjoy each other's company, not that we have to work at that, they really do get along, most of the time at least. When they are older they'll start to do things together, and—like all brothers—they'll argue. They argue now, come to think of it; they'll fight over anything, from who's having the toys to who gets use of the Walkman, but they are only the little spats that all siblings have.

I'm glad to say that neither sees me as a star figure, just because I play before big crowds and I'm often on the telly. They just see me as their dad, who happens to go out from time to time on the rugby field running about with a ball in his hands. 'What's my dad doing out there?' kind of thing. They've grown up with it and it is part of their lives, and it has become a big part of Erika's life.

That's not to say that we're not reminded occasionally that many people look at rugby league players, particularly those in Super League, as stars. I had my own heroes as a Featherstone Rovers supporter when I was a kid, notably the likes of Deryck Fox and Brendan Tuuta. Rovers have had many other great servants over the years, including men like Don Fox, Joe Mullaney, Jim Thompson, Vince Farrar and a host of scrum halves such as Steve Nash and Carl Dooler.

Wakefield Trinity, my present club, have their own legends, including Neil Fox and, of course, the late David Topliss, going right back to the days of the immortal Jonty Parkin in the 1920s. Jonty Parkin was the diminutive international half back with a superb kicking game who caused a sensation by arranging his own transfer to Hull Kingston Rovers. This resulted in the Rugby Football League subsequently changing the rules. There was also the legendary Derek 'Rocky' Turner, the loose forward whose reputation as the enforcer 'par excellence' remains unmatched to this day, half a century on from his heyday.

For all our fame, we do tend to see ourselves as normal blokes and I'm glad about that because rugby league players are generally proud of their reputation for having their feet on the ground. Sometimes you do get reminded that, for many people, we are on a bit of a pedestal. That was brought home to me when we took Brennan and Fletcher horse riding at New Miller Dam, near Wakefield. There was a youngster there that day who was a keen Trinity fan and it really made his day to see me—one of his heroes in the same way, I suppose, as Deryck Fox was for me—suddenly turn up.

That's how it's always been and, I suppose, it will always be the same. Professional sport; like any other form of entertainment whether it's music, the theatre, art or simply the telly, gives people the chance to look up from the routine for an hour or two and, in looking up, they also look up to those who are on that stage. Rugby league players, though, come from a certain mould and they don't usually forget their roots. That, happily, is the case whether they hail from England or from the other side of the world. New Zealanders, for example, are invariably great lads—if a little laid back on occasion—and they were quick to turn up at Brennan's school, at Streethouse, during their Police tour in Autumn 2007.

Mick Amos sorted it—what a great bloke he is—and what a memory of that visit the kids will carry for the rest of their lives, especially of the Haka, which I have to say terrified some of them and which I'll quietly confess put the wind up me a bit as well! Brennan and his pals were scared to death and he needed his holiday with us afterwards at half term to recover. It was, in fact, a break we all needed as one aspect of Super League affecting players with families is that you can't, obviously, take holidays during the summer.

Streethouse is a great school, by the way, and Brennan loves going there. He's been there since October 2006, and the teachers are lovely. Two ladies look after him. One deals with stretches, the physio side of things and his education in the morning, and the other continues with his education in the afternoon while also paying attention to his progress with a standing frame and with his walker. Everyone there is good to him, going out of their way to help and get involved, and he enjoys it, which is such an important factor in anything.

Going to Germany, while so vital, obviously presented problems in respect of Brennan's education. There were also other issues to deal with. The speech therapist, for example, compiled a programme for us to take with us, because that's something they wouldn't be able to deal with at the TheraSuitReha Centre in Ratingen, a small town outside Dusseldorf. Their job at the centre was purely to get him active and moving about, so we'd all his schoolwork to take, and his speech programme. Erika had the responsibility for dealing with everything in Germany and ensuring Brennan didn't fall behind too much with his schooling.

The school was, quite rightly, keen to ensure that Brennan kept up as much as he could, and that remains the case. They've been very good to him at Streethouse, which is adapted for children with special needs, although they won't be able to take any more after Brennan for some reason. We think it may be a funding issue, but it's a pity because they are excellent and there will be kids in the future who will miss out.

They've been marvellous to us; Brennan is more-or-less toilet-trained, and they've kept up the progress with that, and in fact done everything we've asked of them. Debbie Leach, his nursery teacher who is responsible for his statementing, is excellent. The school as a whole couldn't have been more supportive and they've fought our corner in every instance when necessary. Perhaps just as important, the kids there have been fine.

They all shout to him when he goes in although they don't call out 'Brennan!' It's 'Brennan Rooney!', which maybe reflects on me playing for Wakefield. One of his teachers, poor soul, is a Leeds Rhinos fan and they have a bit of banter. She'll say, 'Are Leeds going to win Brennan?'

And he'll say, 'No Daddy Wakey!'

Brennan loves me being a player, in fact rugby league is pretty much his life now and he absolutely loves going to matches. I think, all in all, having him and Fletcher around, with the responsibility for a family, has somehow helped me become a better player.

3

RUGBY ROOTS

They say that if you're lucky enough to have been born in Featherstone you've got rugby league in your genes. They may not be far wrong in my opinion—the village has a proud and, I would imagine, an unmatched history of producing a vast number of players who have gone on to grace the sport, right from the grass roots of the local amateur scene through to the very heights of the international Test and World Cup arena. In fact Featherstone, sometimes described as a set of traffic lights between Wakefield and Pontefract, has often been lauded as the very 'heart' of the sport in this country and considering its size it's amazing how many famous players have emerged from the pit village. Featherstone Rovers, despite having one of the smallest catchment areas in the game, have long enjoyed an amazing record of success. Although the club has never been in the Super League—which is a real bone of contention among their loyal fans and even many folk beyond, some of whom reckon that there is a 'glass ceiling' in place in favour of the so-called 'bigger' clubs—their place in the sport's roll of honour is assured.

This is despite the fact that at one time the entire population of Featherstone, calculated in the 1960s as 14,000, could be packed into Rovers' neat, tidy and compact—and, for the opposition, occasionally intimidating—Post Office Road ground. With gates inevitably lower than their rivals, though, simply because of the lower population on which to draw, Featherstone Rovers have traditionally had to sell leading players on simply to survive, and the system worked well for decades before the 'Bosman' ruling effectively put paid to that avenue of revenue.

Rovers remained at the pinnacle of the sport by making maximum use of a seemingly never-ending conveyor-belt of talent, with top young players simply settling into the boots of stars who had moved elsewhere as if nothing had happened. It was said that if Featherstone needed a new scrum half all the committee had to do was pop along to the nearest mine and shout down the pit shaft. Up would come a new number 7 who could almost be guaranteed to challenge for international honours.

This trend was especially apparent in the 1950s, 1960s and 1970s. Rovers, in their famous and fearsome irregular blue and white hooped shirts, made their first appearance at Wembley in 1952. This was exactly 30 years after becoming a professional club when, under player-coach Eric Batten, and with the legendary Freddie Miller at full back at the age of 35, they took on a Workington Town side which had only been formed in 1945 and which was coached by the immortal Gus Risman. That debut outing in the

Challenge Cup Final ended in an 18–10 defeat, but Featherstone Rovers had arrived. It would be 15 long and arduous years before Rovers again reached Wembley, but there were some near misses during that time, with five semi-final appearances all ending in painful and desperately demoralising defeat.

Featherstone missed out in 1955, losing to Workington—again—13–2, and Town were showing signs of becoming a real nuisance to Rovers' ambitions when they reached Wembley again, at Rovers' expense, in 1958 with an 8–2 verdict. Twelve months later, it was Hull's turn to end the hopes of my home town, with a 15–5 win. A very unlucky three-year spell continued in 1960 when (after Rovers had won 15–0 at Workington in the first round to get a monkey off their backs) Wakefield Trinity put paid to Featherstone's ambitions with an 11–2 victory. Trinity piled on the agony once more in 1962 when, in making a brave assault on 'All Four Cups', they prevailed 9–0 at the penultimate stage.

Wakefield, who went on to beat Huddersfield at Wembley, were only denied a clean sweep—and the chance to emulate Hunslet, Huddersfield and Swinton—when Huddersfield, captained by my great friend and mentor Tommy Smales, won the Championship Final at Odsal in the last game of the season. On that basis, there was no disgrace in losing to such a great side, but missing out in the semi-finals in an era in which the Challenge Cup and an appearance at Wembley was pretty much the be-all and end-all in the domestic game was becoming hard to take.

The importance of the Challenge Cup in that era was illustrated by the size of the crowds for each of those semi-finals. A crowd of 33,499 turned up at Headingley for the 1955 game, and the attendance at Odsal when we faced Workington again in 1958 was 31,517. Twelve months later, 52,131 turned up at Odsal to witness our defeat at the hands of Hull, while the crowd for the game against Wakefield Trinity at the same venue in 1960 was even higher at 55,935. The attendance dipped for the 1962 clash with Trinity, registering at 43,625 which remained healthy enough, and it's significant to those who might say that Featherstone Rovers have always struggled to attract big crowds that in each of those seasons the attendance at the semi-final involving Rovers was the higher of the two games.

With the record of five successive semi-final defeats behind them Rovers fans weren't overly-confident when Featherstone travelled to Fartown, Huddersfield, to take on Leeds in the 1967 semi-final. Leeds, then known as the Loiners, were building a very classy side at the time while Rovers had grafted their way to the last four with a hard-earned victory at Bradford Northern and, in painstaking fashion, earned narrow home wins against Wakefield Trinity and Castleford. But captain Malcolm Dixon inspired his side to a magnificent 16–8 success before a 20,052 'gate'—7,000 more than turned up for the other semi-final, between Barrow and Dewsbury—and the Twin Towers were beckoning again.

Once more, Cumbrians were to represent the barrier between Rovers and the Challenge Cup, but there was to be no disappointment on this occasion. Scrum half Carl Dooler collected the Lance Todd Trophy as the man of the match, working his magic behind a traditionally strong Featherstone pack in which Les Tonks and Graham Harris formed a formidable front row alongside Dixon. Arnie Morgan and Jimmy Thompson provided the graft in the second row and Tommy Smales—the namesake of my mentor—offered the guile at loose forward. The incredible thing is that Rovers won the cup that year in the first season of the 'four-tackle' rule, which worked against their traditional 'stick-it-up-the-jumper' style. Backs such as stand off Mike Smith, three quarters Vaughan Thomas, Keith Cotton, Ken Greatorex and Gary Jordan, together with full back Brian Wigglesworth, who it was discovered later, played with a broken neck in one of the great tales of heroism at Wembley, had the class to see Featherstone through to a 17–12 win. So did coach Laurie Gant, recognised as a true visionary and a man who was said to be years ahead of his time. It may perhaps be significant that Gant already had Wembley experience, having excelled in the second row in the 1952 Challenge Cup Final despite having suffered from flu in the build-up to the match with Workington Town.

For all their successes in the Challenge Cup in the 1950s and 1960s, the 1970s were, perhaps, Featherstone's greatest era, highlighted by the Championship season of 1976–77. Before then,

Rovers featured twice at Wembley, both times under that redoubtable coach Peter Fox, who was also at the helm in the title-winning campaign. Bradford Northern, viewed in many quarters (including at Odsal) as hot favourites, were absolutely demolished in 1973, former Hull KR full back Cyril Kellett kicking a record eight goals from as many attempts in a 33–14 win which was, at the time, the biggest aggregate score at Wembley.

Steve Nash—another of my predecessors in the number 7 shirt—won the Lance Todd Trophy for a typically dynamic and intelligent display but for all Nash's excellence perhaps the most important contribution to the cause came from blind side prop Vince Farrar. I said earlier that rugby league players are, in the main, modest men and I stand by that. Vince, who still gets down to Post Office Road on a daily basis to help out in any way he can, is a smashing bloke and he certainly fits that description.

His opposite number, Kel Earl didn't win the trophy, opting instead to tell the world, his dog and his goldfish in the build-up exactly what he planned to do to Vince. In fine detail. It was a big mistake as Vince, a fine front row man who knew almost everything there was to know about rugby league, went on to have an absolutely superb game, helping set the platform for Rovers to register five impressive tries, one of which he grabbed himself.

One of the best touchdowns—in fact, perhaps the greatest solo touchdown ever claimed at Wembley, and that's saying something—was by right centre Mike Smith, who weaved his way over from deep in his own half for a try which older folk tell me was featured for many years on BBC's *Grandstand* as part of the opening credits. Left centre and captain John Newlove, who had unluckily missed out on an appearance in the 1967 final against Barrow when Laurie Gant opted for the speedier Vaughan Thomas, made up for that disappointment with two outstanding touchdowns in the first 20 minutes, while substitute David Hartley crossed in the closing stages and Nash landed a drop goal.

All this information was passed down to me, by the way of nuggets of collective folklore, as I was growing up in Featherstone. The stories were relayed, perhaps, as a means of sharing in the glory of where we were all from. Although people didn't tend to talk so much about the next year's final, when Rovers lost 24–9 to Alex Murphy's Warrington in what is generally seen as one of the most mean-spirited and ill-tempered finals ever played at Wembley. There's a famous photo of that game, which I suppose sums up the mood, of a Warrington player laying one on the chin of Featherstone hooker John 'Keith' Bridges. Rovers' pedigree was clearly there, though, and the club enjoyed a proud moment three seasons later with its first Championship, heading the old Division One under redoubtable skipper Vince Farrar with 21 victories and two draws from 30 fixtures.

I was only three years old when Featherstone had their next big day and I can't remember much about it, although I suspect I soaked something in. Rovers were no-hopers against cash-a-wash Hull

FC in the 1983 Challenge Cup Final. The Airlie Birds were the biggest odds-on favourites for many years but someone somewhere seemed to have forgotten to tell Featherstone Rovers, who simply turned on the style to register one of the greatest and most unexpected victories in Challenge Cup Final history. Right centre Steve Quinn landed the late penalty—the last of his four goals—that helped notch a famous 14–12 win in which David Hobbs, Rovers coach until recently, was another hero, picking up the Lance Todd Trophy partly for his superbly taken brace of tries. But every one of Featherstone's players, particularly that great servant Peter Smith, were courageous performers that day.

This, then, was the fabulous pedigree, the expectation even, that I was feeding into and drawing from when I started to play at the age of six or seven. I was happily following in the impressive footsteps of my older brother Chris, who excelled with Travellers Saints and played two age groups above me. Chris could, I'm sure, have quite easily made his mark in the higher reaches of the professional game if he'd had half a mind to. Sheffield Eagles were certainly taken by him, and offered him a full time contract after he'd joined their Academy side but—after a lot of soul-searching, it has to be said—he finally decided to turn it down. It was a brave decision to make, many would say, and some might even argue the wrong one, but Chris felt he was making the right choice and I'm sure he still feels the same way now. For him, it was simple. He was completing his apprenticeship as an electrician, had very good prospects, and it was too much of a risk to throw all that away for the possibility, but not the certainty, of a successful career as a Super League player.

For my money, he'd have done well, and I'm sure many other people who had seen him develop over the years feel the same way, but it was a gamble Chris wasn't prepared to take. He wanted to get a trade under his belt, and you can't really blame him at all for that. I think he fell out with the game a little bit; he became interested in girls and other things—not beer (I hope not at that age) although almost every youngster has a couple of cans now and then—but his rugby career went out of the window, you could say. Unfortunately, Chris and I have never played together, but he still manages to squeeze in the odd game now and then, work permitting, with local amateur club Featherstone Lions, before having to sit out the next 10 or so games.

He left one legacy to the game—a scrapbook. We're both fortunate, like so many others, to have a permanent record of our junior days. The scrapbook was not, I hasten to add, something we started ourselves. Doting mothers and grandmothers often like to keep scrapbooks and as soon as Chris started playing our grandma, Edith Rooney, proud of his achievements at Travellers Saints, duly opened one—entitled *Christopher and Jamie's scrapbook*—which makes fascinating reading. Gran regularly continued to paste newspaper cuttings when I started playing, and she conscientiously kept up the habit until fairly recently, when arthritis unfortunately started to get the better of her. It's a great and heart warming record of what we did as youngsters, and one I get out and look at from time to time even now. It sometimes seems like I'm reading about someone else when I look at those old cuttings now and it's a wonder how the reports didn't go to my head. I've always scored plenty of points somehow. Maybe it's a habit as much as anything—if it is, I'm glad that I acquired it early—and the papers, particularly the *Pontefract & Castleford Express*, which has always done the local amateur game proud, faithfully published the reports submitted by proud Travellers Saints coaches.

There was little chance of me being ruined by the repeated eulogies—not with my mum and dad, keen to keep my feet on the ground, around. They were great parents for all three of us—Karla, my sister, as well as Chris and me. They were two totally different people, and in that respect, I suppose that they made a fantastic team. My mam would take up her usual position at the side of the field and set to, hollering her head off, while my dad would always stand behind the sticks taking it all in and not saying a word. When we were on our own, he'd tell me if I played well, or if I'd played badly. Coming from my dad it meant something and I used to take it all on board, largely because he wasn't a shouter and a bawler. After a game my mam, God love her, might say, 'You were bloody rubbish today,' or something like that, and that would be it. My dad might say more or less the same, but he would tell me why. That kind of advice has helped me with what I'm doing today.

They were wonderful days with Travellers and we all enjoyed them, including Karla. It was a family thing and she'd be there, nicely wrapped up if the weather was cold with her hat and scarf on. I'm sure that if she'd been a lad she'd have played rugby as well. I was a kicker even at that stage. I started kicking at six years old and for whatever reason I've always enjoyed it, even during those periods when I've been missing and not doing well. I've normally been the first choice kicker, wherever I've been, and I've always been a strong believer in getting in plenty of practice. I go in early, before training, to practise on my own for a couple of hours or even longer if possible. It's about commitment, pure and simple. I know it's an old adage, but it just happens to be true; the harder you practise, the luckier you get.

Getting plenty of rugby as a youngster doesn't do any harm either, or at least it didn't in my case. I used to play three times a week, often twice in a day. I'd play for the club in the morning and for school in the afternoon, and it never bothered me. I never felt tired, it's something I always enjoyed. When I went to High School they had a rugby team as well. It got to the stage when I could be playing three or four times a week, and my dad was always there. He always booked his shifts so he could watch me play at school. I think I showed a natural aptitude for rugby league, in common with so many other Featherstone lads, and one of my happiest early memories was winning the Junior Sportsman Trophy, a local award publicised by the *Pontefract & Castleford Express*, at the age of eight, in October 1988.

This was, I think, in recognition of a season in which, playing in a strong side, I'd been able to make my mark with plenty of tries. Gran's cuttings start with the mention of a touchdown a year earlier at Crigglestone, where our captain Matthew Grace scored a try and two goals and Dale Richardson touched down in a 16–0 win. A month after that, I was credited with earning five tries in our game against Normanton, and early the following year I grabbed three tries when we hit back from 10–4 down at half time to beat Half Acres in the semi-final of the Castleford and District Under 9s Cup. It's a pattern which I'm glad to say continued through my junior career, helped, I'm sure, by the excellent coaching I received at every age level at Travellers. There's mention of three tries and seven goals for the Castleford Under 11s in a 46–0 win over Wakefield and at the end of that season my Travellers coach, in his end-of-season presentation, said of me:

> He has such pace and awareness of the game. He is a match-winner who can create and score some marvellous tries. However, the most pleasing thing for me is the way he has developed and broadened his reading of the game.
>
> His distribution, running, tackling and

positional kicking has been first class all season. This despite carrying niggling injuries for most of the year. He has truly been the lynchpin of our team performances—our captain, Jamie Rooney. When we have looked to him to produce something special he has invariably done so. He has electric pace, defends strongly and his kicking game is first class. His all-round play this season has been excellent.

I wouldn't mind reading something like that about myself now—nor, I've no doubt, would any other player in Super League and I wonder if some of the lads I played alongside and against in the Under 11s Yorkshire v North West Counties game in 1991 enjoyed similar praise at their own clubs.

I bet they did, looking at some of the names in the programme, which listed youngsters such as Paul Wellens (St Helens), John Stankevitch (Widnes) and Danny Sculthorpe (Oldham) in the North West Counties side, with Karl Pratt (Hunslet), Jamie Rooney, Andrew Lynch (Leeds) and Stuart Dickens (Wakefield) in the White Rose line up. I was at scrum half, which had always been my position, rather than stand off, until I went to Wakefield. I've been in that slot since I was six years of age, but I've tended to operate at stand off since my move to the Wildcats. And yet, at international level, I was selected at seven for the All Golds fixture at Warrington in the autumn of 2007. It can be intriguing how different coaches see players in different ways, there's no doubt it's all part of rugby league's rich tapestry.

Wherever I'm playing I've always had a penchant for drop goals, one of the most satisfying means of scoring if it's done at the right time. There was a signal of my hunger in a couple of late reports, one recording how I helped snatch an 11–10 win over St John Fisher Under 15s, another telling the tale of a drop goal giving us a handy advantage in a 19–17 victory in an Under 16s win at Bingley.

A special memory of my youth and junior years has little or nothing to do with playing the game and everything to do with emulating those Featherstone Rovers heroes of the 1950s, 1960s, 1970s and 1980s by appearing on the major stage of Wembley. In 1993 I was lucky enough to be selected as a ball boy for the Challenge Cup Final between Widnes and Wigan. One of my proudest possessions is the photo of all of us with Castleford referee Russell Smith, who incidentally had the courage and presence of mind that day to send Widnes second row Ritchie Eyres off for a foul tackle. Those days as a junior player with Travellers Saints, and playing for my school teams at St Thomas Junior School and Featherstone High School, were as happy as any in my life. They were, however, little more than ideal preparation for the future, although that future was to take a step in the right direction when I signed for Featherstone Rovers, under the watchful eye of David Ward, in 1996. However, my brother, sister, our mam and I were about to suffer a hammer blow which would throw all our lives into turmoil.

4

MENTORS

I reckon one of the main reasons I was so keen to pile up the points as a junior player—a hunger which, I'm happy to say, has never left me—was the incentive offered by my dad. There will, I've no doubt whatsoever, be more than a few parents reading this book who will have noticed, perhaps to their subsequent and quiet regret, how the prospect of pocketing 25p for each tackle, say, or a quid for every try can suddenly transform their offspring's approach to playing rugby league.

You'll have seen it for yourself, I'm sure. Little Jimmy will have spent three or four months playing for the local Under 8s side, week in, week out, training maybe twice a week as well, and has never seemed to be properly focussed. His attention will drift away from the pitch during matches, he will seem less than interested in bringing down his opposite number and he will lack the extra motivation needed to bust that tackle and score for his side. It's a scenario common the world over and the answer to it is, I'm sure, equally common wherever the game is played. Many a dad, keen to see his lad put in a bit more effort and with all other avenues, including gentle persuasion and something approaching threats, will be reduced to offering a concrete incentive. The amount might vary but in my day as a junior player, in the late 1980s, it was usual for parents to pay their kids 50p for each try.

I don't recall dad offering me anything for tackling—maybe he thought I was okay in that department, which is a view sadly not always held by coaches in my professional career—but he did agree to give me 10p for every goal I kicked. It was a fair amount of money in those days and I'm not sure whether, in real terms, I've ever been better off! The taxman, for a start, didn't get involved, and all I had to spend my well-gotten gains on at the age of eight or nine was beer (of the ginger kind) and women. Okay then, not even women—I wasn't that precocious and was happy to wait for Erika, a bonny local lass whom I met at the age of around 15—which as any bloke will agree left me with even more cash in my pocket. I'm not sure I needed any extra incentive in the first place (I think I have an inbuilt urge to score) but the deal was done, I wasn't going to say no, and I duly set about rattling up the points with some aplomb.

There's no doubt about it, I cost dad a packet over the years. I think I broke the try-scoring record at Travellers one year with 91 touchdowns, and I was probably a bit disappointed not to get to three figures, but he never quibbled. He wasn't one to welsh on his bets, but when I think about it he did seem to be at work a lot that year. On reflection, he must have put in a heck of a lot of overtime just to pay me what I was due. Little things like that are so important in helping encourage a kid to do well and it's sad that dad never got to see me play at professional level. He would have loved to have watched me turning out for Featherstone Rovers, Castleford Tigers and Wakefield Trinity Wildcats, and he'd have been tremendously proud to see me in an international jersey. It wasn't to be, unfortunately, but I've been left with wonderful memories of his unfailing support while I was gravitating through the juniors. Even though he never saw me play beyond that, his influence was undoubtedly the biggest I've had on my career. When I was a kid he used to take me everywhere, he used to buy me my boots, he used to give me advice, in fact he used to do everything. Above all, he was determined that I was going to be brought up in the right way, just as he had. I think that, having recognised that I'd been blessed with some rugby talent, he was equally keen that I should be given every opportunity in rugby league, while still paying proper attention to my studies.

For all that, rugby came first, and he went out of his way to take me to every match and to every training session. That became tougher when we moved to Wakefield, to a village called Horbury. It was important that I continued to play for Travellers in Featherstone, where the coaching was excellent and remains so in the club's modern-day guise as Featherstone Lions, so he took me across twice a week for training and to matches. Nobody ever heard him moan about this. He was always positive about everything he did, especially for his family, and it was abundantly clear that he thoroughly enjoyed watching me play and even train. Dad worked down the pit and he would come home straight from shift work and take me off to training without so much as a grumble. To see his two lads playing rugby put a smile on his face and for that matter it put a smile on my mum's face as well.

In fact I think he got just as much pleasure from it as I did. Although I'll always regret that he was denied the opportunity to see me play as a professional, fortune did allow him the joy of seeing me sign for Featherstone Rovers. That, I know, was one of his proudest moments. He'd not played much rugby himself, just a bit at school I think, but he knew plenty about the game, he could assess a player, and he recognised quickly that I had potential. Potential is one thing, but it has to be realised, and that's where parents such as my dad are so important.

While he certainly got so involved because he enjoyed it, his main motivation was to help me to make the most of my abilities, with no stone left unturned in the attempt. He and mam felt just the same way about my elder brother Chris, who I believe could have done well in the professional game if he'd been so inclined, and our sister Karla. The other thing that maybe helped persuade dad, a man who expected high standards of behaviour, to really get behind us in sport was that, while we were training or playing, we were keeping out of bother. This is one aspect of youth and junior rugby, and of any other sport for that matter, that perhaps gets overlooked far too often. The devil makes work for idle hands, so the proverb goes, and while you're sweating your way round the training pitch, or battling to keep the opposition away from your tryline, you're keeping well away from trouble.

Dad would be at Sevens tournaments all day, helping make an event of it, rather than just chucking me in with the other parents and clearing off. He never ever did that, he wasn't the type. Most weekends, Chris would play in the morning and I'd play in the afternoon, or so it seemed, so we'd all troop off to both games as a family. He and mum must have spent thousands of pounds in petrol money and buying us new boots. That's something all parents do, and I'll do the same for my children too. Brennan won't be able to play rugby but I'm sure he'll home in on some abiding interest, while Fletcher is already showing signs that he might follow in my footsteps. He certainly likes to kick a rugby ball and, even at two years old, it's not too early to pick up some good habits.

One game in particular stands out in my memory from my time at Travellers—not the match itself so much, but the build-up—as an illustration of dad's supportive approach. We were playing away at Bingley, near Keighley on the outskirts of Bradford, and for whatever reason—I was probably struggling to get out of bed—we were late arriving at the meeting point in Featherstone. Everyone had gone when we arrived at the Travellers ground and I was in a real state, the way only a kid can be, thinking I'd missed out on a game. Dad was having none of it and we set off to Bingley, which is one of those places (as anyone who has been to Keighley's ground will attest) which isn't that straightforward to get to, with no direct route. I cried all the way there, which can't have made it any easier for my harassed dad, who all the while was attempting to calm me down whilst reading the road signs and watching for other traffic. Somehow, though, we got there and I was able to play the full second half. It was worth it because I ended up scoring a couple of tries, once I found my legs, which helped us win a closely fought game. At that age you don't have any nerves, you just get changed in the car and go out and play; I sometimes wish it was like that now. But the mere thought of missing the game was, for me at that age, heartbreaking.

There's not a day that passes that I don't think about my dad. He meant a great deal to me, more than I realised when he was around if I'm honest, and I just wish that he was here to see me play now, but that's life. I'm sure he's watching over us all, though. If he is, I think he'll be as proud as my mum is, and we're equally proud of him.

Away from rugby, he brought us up with the right kind of discipline when we needed it, and that's certainly stood us all in good stead, Chris, Karla and me. He was a caring father who was there for his kids, whom he loved, and he worked all hours God sent to make sure we had everything we wanted. If it's true that only the good die young—well, the proof is there in my dad's case.

It was just a normal weekday afternoon, and Karla and I had come home from school ready to do our homework and settle into our usual evening routines. I think I was due to train that night. Chris had started work by then, and he wasn't due back for a while, and mum was also at work. I went upstairs to dad's bedroom and he was laid on the floor. I just assumed he was asleep, I don't know why I thought that. Perhaps anything else was unthinkable for a normal 15-year-old. Karla went upstairs and she started screaming. I thought, 'Oh God, something's up,' and I phoned the ambulance straight away. It turned out that a blood vessel had burst in dad's head while he was watching the telly. The signs weren't good.

It's strange how you can react to incidents such as that, and I'm sure many other people will have noticed the same thing. I used to work on a milk round and I was due to help out the following day. I always turned up, and I went along as usual. I was on the round when one of mum's friends Karen Raybould, phoned the milkman and said she'd have to collect me and take me to hospital. Being the lad that I was, and I suppose still am, I wanted to finish my job first. It was two hours later that we completed the round and I was taken by Karen and Charlie Raybould to Pinderfields, where dad had been transferred from Pontefract. I was told that he was dying. Thinking about the state I'd seen him in when he left the house, I wasn't expecting good news really. I thought that was the end of the world. For months afterwards I just expected him to be there, and he wasn't, and it was difficult for all of us. It rocked me for a while, but I had to try to move on.

The whole family was around dad's bedside, and they turned the machine off while I was there. I think they had been waiting for me to arrive before they made the decision. Until we found out about our Brennan's condition, that was the worst moment of my life. It's something I wouldn't wish on anyone. You could say it's a lot worse regarding Brennan, because he's got the rest of his life to lead. It brought everything back when the news of his cerebral palsy came through—I felt sick, as I had done when my dad died, and I wondered what we were going to do.

My dad was an only child and we haven't really got a big family. Not, that is, until I met Erika, who has family coming out of her ears. Her brother, Lee, has six kids already, so we have a wide and integrated support base. It was difficult in the days, weeks and months following dad's death. mum took us all on holiday a few months later, because we always used to go away. She didn't want us to move out of our routine, she wanted us to carry on as normal, or as normally as we could, and she was absolutely right to do that. It was still a difficult trip. I never want my kids to see their parents dying so young.

Dad was just 42 years old when he died in 1996, which is no age to die. There can't be a good age for a child to be when a parent passes away and I suppose being 15 was as bad an age as any. I was on the verge of being an adult and I needed guidance. I don't mind admitting that I struggled.

It was hard to accept and I couldn't really see any future. I was only young but I started drinking, and I think I was in danger of going off the rails. mum and Erika will tell you I was a real pain, and that my dad's death really changed me. I'd just started seeing Erika, who unfortunately never got to meet my dad, and I'm still sad about that. I found the experience to be devastating and, reflecting on that period, I was on a downwards spiral. I'm not sure how far I would have tumbled if I hadn't been lucky enough to have a few people around me who, in a way, took over the role of a father figure.

Nobody could replace my dad, and no one ever will, but I've been incredibly fortunate to have a few blokes in my life who have offered vital guidance at important times. First among them is Tommy Smales, to whom I've already referred. Jon Sharp was another. Jon was sacked by Huddersfield as I was writing this book, after doing a fine job, in my opinion, in recent seasons. In addition to helping make Huddersfield a force to be reckoned with in Super League, he guided them to the Challenge Cup Final in 2006 and I wasn't the slightest bit surprised by his success.

He knows the game through and through—being a Featherstone lad, he would—and I can vouch for his man-management skills, to which I owe a great deal. Jon Sharp, who has also coached at Batley and St Helens, was the Featherstone Rovers Academy boss when I signed at Post Office Road, and I thank my lucky stars for that. I was still playing at Travellers Saints but training with the Academy and he could see that I was in a state. He didn't mess about, he just had a quiet word with me and put me straight. He told me that I had an excellent chance of having a good career in the game and that I'd be letting my father down if, after all the effort he'd put in, I let the opportunity go to waste. Jon hit the right nerve, and his message brought me back to reality. He'd played at Featherstone, of course, so apart from him being my coach I automatically had a lot of respect for him and I was prepared to listen. You respect what someone like that says and take their advice on board. That little chat, which amounted to a short, sharp shock, really triggered me to knuckle down again. Whatever I achieved, or might still achieve, in the sport is partly down to him and I'm grateful.

He must have seen the potential in me, he knew what was going on in my life at the time, and he wanted to put me right. I thought hard about what he said and I quickly realised he was right; I didn't want my life to be a waste and, after all the years of my dad doing what he did for me, it would have been very disappointing for me to just throw it all away. I've seen it myself, how people start drinking and think rugby is just a hobby, but I've got a decent career out of it now, and it's enabling me to bring up two children with my partner. If I'd thrown all that away, life would have been so much different. I wouldn't change my life for the world.

My mum, like most women in Featherstone, has a forthright personality—we wouldn't have her any other way. It must be something, handed down over the generations, to do with grinding out an existence in a strong community dominated by the local pit. She had—still has—a loud gob on her, and she never holds anything back. It's one of the many things she has in common with Erika which I admire both of them for. Although, as other Featherstone lads will agree, this can be a shade embarrassing sometimes. mum used to get very excited on the touchline when I was a junior player, and some of what she shouted made sense. Some of it didn't, though, and I'd often blank it off. You don't always want to hear it when someone's shouting like that and there are times— nearly always in fact—when you'd prefer people to be calmer. But she helped me a lot as well, and I always valued her support. Above all, she got me involved with Tommy Smales, who owned the Travellers.

Tommy had been a fine player in his day, having captained the Huddersfield side that won the Championship in 1962, later joining the re-formed Bradford Northern in 1964 and immediately steering the fledgling side to a shock victory over red hot favourites Hunslet in the 1965 Yorkshire Cup Final. He went on to coach Castleford at Wembley in 1970 and 1971 and, in his well-earned retirement, he is a physio, treating players such as Barrie McDermott, Paul Sculthorpe, Lee Gilmore, Leslie Vainikolo, Gareth Raynor, the list goes on, at his Featherstone home. Above all, he's simply Tommy Smales, and he's been a massive, positive influence on my life. If it wasn't for mum, I'd have probably never got to know him. And, while Jon Sharp was a vital figure in getting me back on the straight and narrow, I certainly don't think I'd have got to where I am today without Tommy's help.

My dad, Jon Sharp and Tommy Smales were all key male role models in my formative years. I didn't really meet Tommy until after dad died, obviously I knew he owned the pub but I was too young to go into pubs then. I think I started training with Tommy when I was about 17 or 18, possibly after my mum had a word with him. She told him that I seemed to be going off the rails a bit and Tommy took me under his wing, which was a wonderful thing to do. Obviously he could never replace my dad but he has pretty much taken over that role really. I trained with him nearly every day when I was full time at Featherstone, did a lot of work with him, and just became really close to him. To this day I still see a lot of him.

I've had to look after him sometimes; in fact he injured himself a few years ago training with me, and the upshot is that I'm still treating him. We were running up and down hills in Featherstone— it was belting it down but he wouldn't let me have the day off—and he fell flat on his back. He couldn't move for 10 minutes; he'd winded himself and twisted his knee. This was nine or 10 years ago and I'm still treating him to this day, forcing a big iron bar against his knee. He'll treat me, then I have to treat him 10 minutes after we've finished—there's something wrong somewhere about this arrangement!

Tommy gets along to my games as often as he

can (which means he watches nearly every game) then he sits down with me and we go through the videos. He'll pick up what I'm doing right and what I'm doing wrong, and he'll point me in the right direction. It's something he's done with me for quite a few years now, starting from when I was at Featherstone, and the insights he offers are perceptive and important. He played a long time ago, of course, and the game has changed so much in the intervening period, so there are occasions when he may say something that at first hearing may not appear that relevant. But his madness invariably makes a lot of sense if you know what I mean. In the end, he's just looking out for me and I've not a shred of doubt that I owe all my career, as it stands now, essentially to him. Without Tommy Smales I don't think I'd have been able to leave Featherstone, because I wouldn't have been as good a player. He's worked on everything with me; during the years when I was at Rovers, when I was training on my own, I used to train a lot with him. I owe him a great deal; he's been a big part of my career, and of my life.

5

BREAKING THROUGH

Featherstone is a closely-knit community famous above all for producing rugby league players. It's always meant a great deal to local lads to play for the Rovers. The former pit village has probably produced more professionals—and good ones at that—than any other district of comparable size. Although I was too young to be aware of it at the time (at only three years of age) that fact was vividly illustrated when Featherstone beat mighty Hull FC in the Challenge Cup Final at Wembley in 1983. The victory, one of the greatest upsets of all time at the famous stadium, was all the more remarkable for the fact that Hull, that day, had more Featherstone lads in their ranks than they had players from the east coast—not to mention coach Arthur Bunting.

Achievements of that kind tend to enter the annals of folklore, so it meant everything to me when I put pen to paper for the club that had paraded my boyhood heroes, Deryck Fox and Brendan Tuuta. And it was a choice that I never regretted for a moment. I owe Rovers a great deal for kick-starting my career as a professional rugby league player, and for helping to give me the grounding as a sportsman which has stood me well now for over a decade. It seems an age ago since David Ward—then in charge at Post Office Road—signed me on. He was a charismatic figure and an obvious early inspiration although, to be fair, as an Academy player I didn't have very much direct contact with him.

This was perhaps just as well, all things considered. Ward had made his redoubtable name as a player as a whole-hearted and courageous hooker at Leeds, whom he captained. He continued to adopt a hands-on approach as a coach, where he liked to remain one of the lads as much as he could. In fact, I think he found it very difficult to accept that he was no longer a player, which is understandable for someone who offered so much commitment as the Loiners' skipper, and he just loved to get physically involved in training. Whether he'd done that in his previous coaching roles, firstly with Hunslet, whom he guided to promotion from Division Two in 1986–87, then with Leeds, whom he took very close to the First Division championship a couple of years later, I don't know. I imagine from what I saw at Featherstone that he had more than a few Hunslet and Leeds players looking over their shoulders during his time at the helm at, firstly, Elland Road and then Headingley. He loved to get his tracksuit and boots on and get out on the pitch or training paddock, where he could immerse himself in the rough-and-tumble, and there was nothing he liked better than knocking the younger players (let's face it, they were all younger than him) about.

You'd run at him, thinking he was an old man, and he'd put you on your arse, showing you clearly that he could still hack it. He liked to be involved, he was like that as a player and he carried that on to the coaching side as well, and all credit to him for that.

I didn't have all that much to do with Wardie when I was with Rovers. I was focussing, at that time, on serving my apprenticeship with the Academy but it wasn't until 1998, after Ward had gone when Australian Steve Simms had been in charge for a year, that I eventually made my debut. I made four appearances that season, two as a substitute, landing a couple of goals in the 48–24 victory at St Esteve in the Tres Tournois tournament, a competition designed for leading French sides and top English teams in Division One. This was played after we'd lost, agonisingly, to Wakefield Trinity—of all teams—24–22 in the Division One Play-off Final at Huddersfield, when a place in Super League had been at stake.

That defeat put paid to my early hopes of playing in the top flight with Featherstone Rovers—with hindsight, it dashed them entirely— and my full debut in a solely British competition came the following year after Kevin Hobbs had taken over from Simms. What a day that was. If I thought beforehand, in my fond imagination, that the headlines would hopefully focus on a promising debut for local product Jamie Rooney in a league fixture at struggling Doncaster, I was sadly mistaken. I have mixed memories of that memorable afternoon. Although I scored a try, we lost to the Dons, and that was bad news because they were bottom of the league. It was hard to take but the fans, or a minority of them, didn't react very well at all. The unexpected defeat led to a section of Featherstone's support, frustrated at what they felt had been a series of poor performances by Rovers, turning on Hobbs' wife and family, who had been sitting in the stands.

Not surprisingly, Kevin Hobbs was very upset and stepped down. It was hard to blame him but I have to admit that, as a young player and still wet behind the ears, I didn't quite know what to make of it all. I was aware, living in the village as I did, that the first team hadn't been playing too well, and it was no secret that Kevin was under a bit of pressure. But I never expected his family to get abused and I don't think anyone else did. You don't need that, as a player or as a coach. It can be hard enough, hurtful even, for wives and girlfriends, and other family members or friends, sitting in the stands and overhearing criticisms, valid or unjustified, of their loved ones.

Erika, as it happens, always sits in the clubhouse at Belle Vue, largely because it's easier in there for Brennan and Fletcher. That's just as well because I don't know what she'd do if she heard anybody having a go at me. The ensuing scene might not turn out to be too pleasant; I can tell you that she's not one to hold her words back. Spectators don't always seem to realise that players don't go out meaning to miss a tackle. Nobody intends to drop the ball, everyone simply wants to do their best.

Some days a player doesn't play at the peak of his game, for whatever reason. It isn't possible for anyone to be at 100 per cent all the time, and that's a fact which unfortunately some fans can't appreciate. Nor do they always realise that players who may appear to be having a quiet game or taking the wrong option could merely be acting in accordance with instructions.

Every coach I've played under, and there have been a few now, has had some stick at some time or another. The list includes each of my bosses at Post Office Road, with Peter Roe—a real stalwart for me—Ian Fairhurst and Andy Kelly all figuring in the roster. Things don't always go according to plan and as often as not it just cannot be helped. The result goes against you, and that's it. There was an instance in my first regular season, in 1999, when we travelled to Hunslet Hawks in the Northern Ford Premiership play-offs, with a place in Super League the ultimate prize. We were 9–0 up at half time and appeared to be coasting to victory. We'd been well on top in the first 40 minutes, we were good value for our lead, and it looked as though we had booked our place in the semi-finals.

Maybe we thought the job had been done and took victory for granted, but it didn't pan out our way. The Hawks, with livewire hooker Richard Pachniuk increasingly calling the shots, somehow turned the game around in the last 40 minutes and ended up winning 17–9, ending our hopes of Super League for a second successive year. We were left on the sidelines watching the rest of the action, although the victory over us didn't do Hunslet much good in the long run. The Hawks went on to beat Widnes in the qualifying semi-final, not without some controversy, and subsequently disposed of Dewsbury in the Grand Final. But the compact South Leeds Stadium was deemed by Rugby League bosses to be unsuitable for Super League, primarily because of its 2,500 capacity. So Hunslet weren't allowed to go up, even though they looked at other venues (including Post Office Road and the Jungle, Castleford, neither of which passed muster at Red Hall, which was a little odd given that the Tigers were already in Super League).

With hindsight, it was maybe no bad thing from a personal perspective that Rovers had failed to make it into the top flight. I was able to continue my development at a more leisurely pace in the less exacting arena of the Northern Ford Premiership, and my game was moving along nicely. By February 2000 coach Peter Roe, who together with my Dad, Tommy Smales and Jon Sharp can take a lot of credit for much of my progress, was publicly lauding my abilities and suggesting that Super League would eventually be a fitting arena for me. He was quoted in the *Rugby Leaguer* as stating: 'By his own admission, Jamie is not yet ready for Super League, but it won't be long before he is. We want to hang onto him but if someone from Super League came in for him, we would not hold him back. Jamie is probably the most dedicated player I have worked with.' That was high praise and much appreciated from a man like Roe, who had a long and successful career as a hard-bitten but skilful centre who, through injury, spent his later years effectively using only one leg.

With the help of his unfailing encouragement and wise guidance, I continued to progress and in January 2001 became the fastest player to reach 100 points in a season in Rovers' history, passing the milestone with 14 points from a try and five goals in the 26–14 victory over Hunslet on the last day of the month. This was despite having one goal disallowed in that match, one touch judge raising his flag but the other one siding with the referee in vetoing my effort.

Roe, by this stage, was pushing my case for inclusion in the England team, and not only because of my penchant for points. My Featherstone boss, citing my ability to work with my forwards and provide an effective link with the backs as a key factor, was reflecting on a year which had gone well for me, maybe better than even I had expected. I scored 25 points for the second successive year against Oldham in March, highlighting a satisfactory start to the campaign, and earned praise from *League Express* following our 28–8 victory over Hull KR a month later—a success which got us back into gear after a surprise defeat at the hands of Rochdale Hornets.

The following month, I was on hand to send Matt Bramald over for a winning try five minutes from time in the narrow victory over Doncaster, after having scored all our other points with a try and four goals—and our good fortune continued against Workington Town. The Cumbrians, who had not won on our patch since 1954, were beaten 58–8 and I'd scored 18 points by half time, with two tries and five goals, before having to retire with ankle trouble. I struggled on my return a shade, coming off second best against the wily veteran Mike Ford in our clash with Oldham, but bounced back to something like my top form in the play-off semi-final victory over Widnes Vikings, picking up the man of the match award.

It meant a lot to me when I was awarded the Steven Mullaney Memorial Trophy at the end of the season as Featherstone Rovers' Player of the Year. Steven, of course, was the youngster who was tragically killed in a car accident less than a year after having thrilled TV viewers with his try, and his tearful celebrations, in the Schoolboys Under 11s curtain raiser to the 1986 Challenge Cup Final at Wembley. It's only right that Rovers recognise the son of Terry, who has worked hard for Featherstone in many capacities for many years, and Terry's wife Denise and daughter Lauren. I was also delighted to be recognised as the Northern Ford Premiership Young Player of the Year for 2000, and to cap it all Erika was a finalist in the *Wakefield Express'* 'Look of 2000' competition—as I'd have expected as she's always been gorgeous. It was round about then that I scored 21 points in a 37–6 win at Batley on my mum, Karen's, birthday. So things were looking pretty good, although there are always reminders in this world that others are not so fortunate.

I eventually became the only player in the

squad at Featherstone to be able to devote myself entirely to rugby league. It's part of a sportsman's role, particularly for full time players, to offer some comfort and solace to people who are suffering from a serious illness, and I was a regular visitor to Pontefract General Infirmary, where I would try to cheer up sick children. One visit, in late 1999, was to see seven-year-old Jake Sherburn, a lovely little lad who was suffering from cerebral palsy and a deformed heart. Brave Jake was also partially paralysed down his left side. Little did I suspect, as I posed with him for photographs, that a few years later I would be standing alongside my own son, in exactly the same way, for the media.

Meanwhile, rugby league has always been a hard game, and playmakers have long been a target for the 'hatchet men'. It's always been part of the sport, even if some old timers tell me that the game has been cleaned up a lot in recent years. I suppose the fact that most matches these days are televised or videoed, at least in Super League, makes it difficult for those who like the 'darker side' to get away with their indiscretions. Incidents still occur, though, and there's no doubt about it; as a half back I have to expect a bit of extra attention. This was highlighted in an edition of *Rugby League Raw*, the TV series which focussed on the Northern Ford Premiership and which introduced the innovation of a camera—and a microphone—into the dressing rooms.

It was a controversial concept, largely because of the industrial language used occasionally by players and coaches, but there was one memorable moment (for me at any rate) when we were playing Widnes. One of the Hulme brothers, I'm not sure if it was Paul or David, was heard to say of me, 'Don't let that little twat run around'. That, of course, was a routine instruction, and fair comment, but things were definitely getting hotter for me out on the pitch. I had an interesting time in a fixture with Batley, who had Gary Barnett at scrum half. Gary was a wily old campaigner, brought up in the hard school, and he introduced me to an interesting little tactic which was perhaps a throwback to the era of contested scrums. He threw the ball into the pack in such a way that it bounced out and I had to dive on it. And he then stamped on me. I thought that was a bit out of order and I said as much at the time. As it happened, Gary joined Featherstone later and I got to know him pretty well. He's a smashing bloke and after a while he revealed that he was just trying to rough up a youngster.

The 'roughing up' was, on reflection, beginning to intensify. It appeared that as my reputation began to spread, teams were attempting to intimidate me and put me off my game or, perhaps, put me out of a match entirely in some instances. Peter Roe, who had never been one to hang back as a player, had a real blast after a game at Widnes in which the Vikings' Lee Birdseye was sent off 14 minutes from time in our 28–22 win. Birdseye had been given his marching orders for a high tackle on me and Peter had a word with RFL Referees' Controller Greg McCallum about it. He said: 'Rooney's kicking game is proving to be a real thorn in opposing teams' sides and obviously he is a player an opposition coach will highlight. But once the ball has left his hand there is absolutely no point in doing what we saw on Sunday. It was ridiculous.'

It was more than ridiculous in a game against York. I had my jaw broken in the fifth minute, although I don't think I realised it was as serious as that at the time. In fact I stayed on the pitch and picked up the man of the match award. What happened was that I'd kicked through, was chasing the ball and got an elbow, belonging to Alan Pallister, in my face. It wasn't good and I'm not having a pop at Pallister, it's something that we all accept is part and parcel of the game although, happily, it's not quite as prevalent as it used to be. And in all fairness, that was the only injury I sustained during my time at Featherstone. I rarely missed a game, so perhaps I was lucky.

Maybe the fact that I was virtually an ever-present was a factor in my being made Featherstone's team captain early in 2001. Danny Evans, one of the best blokes it's possible to have the pleasure to meet in this game, remained club captain, which was a good move on Rovers' part, and it was celebration time for me in the New Years' Day fixture with Doncaster, with two tries and five goals coming my way in a 34–4 victory. I was very happy at Post Office Road but it was gratifying, for all that, to hear that Super League clubs were showing interest in me. No one has his ears closer to the ground in this sport than that doyen of gossip columnists, Dave 'Nosey' Parker of *League Weekly*. 'Nosey' wrote at the time for the *Rugby Leaguer*, and was clearly onto something that even I didn't know about when he remarked in his column at the end of January:

The Rovers' 20-year-old skipper, a product of the club's Academy side, is yet another scrum half of the famous Post Office Road conveyer belt, following on from the likes of Joe Mullaney, Don Fox, Carl Dooler, Terry Hudson, Steve Nash and Deryck Fox.

According to coach Peter Roe, Rooney is so mature and dedicated to his game that he will go all the way. In the past couple of weeks Batley chief executive Ron Earnshaw and Keighley coach Steve Deakin have simply drooled over just one aspect of his play—his kicking game. Ron told me: 'He put in six telling kicks and from each of them they scored a try.' Roe said: 'He completely lives for the game. In the morning he either comes down to the ground to practise his goalkicking, work out in the gym or go down to his mentor, Tommy Smales, who is now a recognised top masseur. He then sleeps in the afternoon and is ready for our three training sessions of an evening. Jamie has grown two inches since I first clapped eyes on him, and is almost six feet tall, which is big for a scrum half, but in no way does it affect his ability, it just enhances it. He has a nice turn of pace, probes well, brings players onto the ball, loves to take on the line of defenders and is an accurate goal-kicker. He is definitely Super League material and, very soon, international material. It needs the GB camp, in readiness for Australia, to be pulling him in now and not waiting until August or September, when they have squad sessions. It will take a six-figure sum to see him on his way.'

Phew! Against that backdrop it wasn't surprising, I suppose, that the big clubs were hovering, but I was determined to make my way, if at all possible, into Super League with my beloved Featherstone Rovers. The journalists were now taking extra interest in my future and it wasn't long before Parker's colleague at the *Rugby Leaguer*, Phil Hodgson, popped down to Post Office Road to grill me over my plans.

I fended him off with the best defence of all— the truth. 'I'm committed to Featherstone Rovers, pure and simple,' I told him. 'Obviously I am ambitious, and I am determined to play in Super League next season. My plan is for that, hopefully, to be with Featherstone Rovers and that's as far as it goes right now.' For the moment, I was happy to try to take Rovers into the top flight, and my good form continued, especially with the boot. I landed six goals in what was described as a 'spiteful' 28–14 win at Sheffield, who were of course coached by Mark Aston, one of my predecessors in a number 7 shirt at Featherstone. Aston, it has to be said, was for whatever reason

My sister Karla, my brother Christopher and me looking trendy.

Yorkshire Team under 9s, 1988 (I'm second from right on the back row).

Under 9s winning the Cas and District Trophy against Redhill at Castleford Tigers ground.

Travellers Saints under 11s.

School captain (bottom row, fourth from right) at St Thomas Middle School.

Me and my good mate Dave Raybould with Dennis Betts and Phil Clarke of Wigan at the School of Excellence for Rugby League.

Cas and District Final winners 1991–92, me with coach John Newlove, the former Featherstone Rovers and Hull FC stand off.

Signing my first professional contract with Featherstone Rovers with mum, Karen, and dad, Kevin, in 1995.

Trying to get Featherstone Rovers going.

©RLphotos.com

Playing in my final season for my local team Featherstone Rovers before joining Wakefield Trinity Wildcats.   ©*RLphotos.com*

Going over for one of many of my tries scored for Featherstone Rovers.   ©RLphotos.com

Adding another conversion in the Rovers colours.

Trying to create something for Rovers with my mate Richard Chapman in support.
©*RLphotos.com*

given a tough time by a section of the fans at Post Office Road, who can unfortunately be a bit impatient—and even worse on occasions, such as the time a few of them tore up a section of the seating at Gateshead.

I landed 12 goals, but didn't score a try, in a 92–2 win over York and it was during that period that I was given a bit of advice by coach Ian Fairhurst, who assisted Peter Roe before taking over in his own right. Ian suggested that I should learn to kick with both legs, and that I should get in some practice with my left foot. I wasn't so sure it was a good idea, although I fully accept that Ian's intentions were good. He wanted me to have more options in open play, and in kicking for goal, as the 'round the corner' style can narrow the target considerably when attempting conversions or penalties from the 'wrong' side. I thought about his proposal long and hard, and it certainly had a lot of merit, in fact he may well have been right. In the end, though, I decided against it. I didn't want to be ordinary with my left leg, so I opted to focus on being as good as I could be with my right leg.

Whether I made the correct decision or not, I'll never know. I have heard subsequently, though, the story of Geoff Gunney, the legendary Hunslet second row forward, who was a very good goalkicker when he signed at Parkside in the early 1950s. Gunney could land them from anywhere, but his style was ungainly to say the least. So the coach, the equally legendary Jack Walkington, took the 16-year-old to one side and taught him how to kick properly. It worked a treat in that

Gunney's style was improved dramatically; his action was a dream to behold. The only problem was that he'd lost his accuracy and, sadly, he never really got it back. So perhaps the lesson is that if it ain't broke, don't try to fix it.

Sticking totally with my tried and trusted right pin, I kept on chipping away at the record books, typified by a 20-point haul at Keighley involving three tries and four goals, the *League Express'* Chris Westwood commenting: 'Jamie Rooney was the game star, doing what he does best, rattling up the points.' I bettered that total with 22 points, from two tries and seven goals, in a 46–40 success over Hull KR and a fixture against Barrow in 2002 approached with two records in sight. Steve Quinn's career record of 1,210 points, registered between 1976 and 1988, was within striking distance, as was the points-in-a-season record of 391 posted by Martin Pearson in 1992–93. We won 45–20 and my tally of 21 points—from two tries, six goals and a drop goal—was enough to take me into the record books on two counts. That was a special moment and I'll always be proud of the twin achievements.

I've never looked back since I left Rovers but I know I owe a lot to my home town club Featherstone; they signed me on and gave me my opportunity as a young kid. A lot of clubs didn't really want to take a punt on me but Featherstone gave me my big chance, for which I'll always be grateful. They signed me on as a junior, put me through their impressive Junior Academy system and developed me into the player that I am today.

Without Rovers I probably wouldn't be where I am now. I'll never forget my roots, Featherstone is where I'm from and they are my local team.

You never know, I might end up back at Post Office Road, which was recently renamed the Chris Moyles Stadium in honour of the Radio One presenter, at the close of my career. Obviously I want to play at the highest level for as long as I can, and go out on a high really. I know a lot of blokes who have been very good players and who should have retired but opted to carry on for too long, giving themselves a bad name in the end. If they'd finished at the top it would have been different; as soon as I start dipping in form, that's when the time will have come for me to call it a day. But, all things being equal, I would love to give the last few of my good years to Featherstone Rovers.

6

SURPLUS TO REQUIREMENTS

Having a sense of perspective is probably not too common in sport. Sportsmen tend to be inward looking, isolated and attach far too much importance to what has or hasn't happened with a ball. Rugby league players are better than most and generally have their feet on the ground, unlike soccer players who sometimes give the impression that they are losing touch with reality. Christiano Ronaldo, for example, might regret what he said (although I'm aware, as a sportsman myself, that he may never have said it or that it could have been taken out of context) during the tug-of-war for his services involving Manchester United and Real Madrid. Ronaldo compared himself to a 'slave' which enraged a lot of people, who pointed out that this insulted the many thousands, millions even, who really are living as slaves today.

It's an example, I suppose, of a loss of perspective, and it happens when people like footballers are wrapped in cotton wool. Very few, if any, rugby league players fall into the same trap and events of the last few years have certainly helped me avoid this. Brennan's issues have helped me focus more on what's important, which isn't to say that I don't take my rugby league seriously any more. I certainly do; but as a parent, and particularly as the father of a child who needs extra care, I'm perhaps much more aware than I used to be that sport isn't a matter of life or death. I can roll with the tide a lot more these days, although that's not to say that I haven't experienced a few setbacks in rugby league, all of which have hopefully made me a stronger person and a better player.

There are, of course, sportsmen who have to go through their travails under a stronger spotlight than I have to face. Ronaldo is one of them, and so is David Beckham, who is always at the centre of a media storm (or so it seems) and who was regularly in the news as I laboured away at this book. There was a lot of fuss and debate over the decision of incoming England soccer coach Fabio Capello not to grant Beckham his 100th cap when the side played Croatia in the Italian's first game in charge. Sure enough in the remarkable saga that is the Beckham story, the former Manchester United star somehow recovered from that perceived snub to regain the captain's armband in the friendly fixture with Trinidad and Tobago. As with so many issues involving Beckham, you wouldn't make it up, but I did feel for him as a sportsman, and as one who clearly loves playing for his country, when he missed out initially on the chance of reaching a century of international appearances.

Top players in every sport are dropped and although Beckham has bounced back I thought it was a bit harsh not to give him his 100th cap. People were saying that he shouldn't have been selected because he wasn't playing very well. That may have been the case, but I disagreed with the stance, largely because of everything he has done over the years for England. It wouldn't have hurt anyone to have brought him on for 20 minutes or so, especially as he's not lost much in terms of ability; class is always there. If he's in the England side he's playing with better players than he is over in America, which would bring out the best in him. He deserved his 100th cap, when it eventually came, and I think the entire country wanted him to get it.

Another high-profile figure, Andrew Flintoff— perhaps Beckham's equivalent in the world of cricket—hit the headlines for all the wrong reasons over the 'pedalo' incident during the World Cup in the West Indies. I thought the treatment he was subjected to, which amounted to trial by media almost, was over the top and unwarranted. Any sportsman, having lost, is a bit down and it doesn't hurt anyone to let their hair down. The media, though, latch onto anything. Cricket is a high-profile sport and everyone seemed to get into Flintoff's ribs. I felt sorry for him. The truth is that rugby players get up to tricks like that all the time but because our game, by comparison, isn't so high profile, they don't find themselves subsequently plastered all over the papers. Although a number of union players, admittedly unnamed, discovered otherwise on their tour of New Zealand in 2008 in an alleged incident which had more serious overtones than simply falling into the sea.

We're better for that. The Flintoff incident was blown up out of all proportion; if a rugby player, of either code, had done the same thing it would probably have been treated as little more than having a laugh. Every time players in certain sports go out for a drink it's in the papers; but they're sportsmen, and they have to unwind sometimes. Some things can't be condoned, but surely it should be okay for players just to have a drink. They're only young blokes after all, which is forgotten far too often. Nothing similar has happened to me thank goodness—I don't drink that much anyway, as it happens, John Kear has really drilled it into us at Wakefield Trinity Wildcats how overindulgence can affect your performance and I buy into that.

I have had a few setbacks during my time as a professional, some of them high profile.

One of the most memorable was the fiasco over my transfer—non-existent transfer, to be more accurate—from Featherstone Rovers to Widnes in late 2001 and early 2002. The saga revolved around a marked difference of opinion about my worth. Professional sportsmen can sometimes feel like they are little more than a piece of meat and that more or less summed up my own reaction when I saw my value, the respective opinions of Widnes, Featherstone and, ultimately, the Rugby Football League's Tribunal, floated in public. Taking my lead from Ronaldo, and hoping not to attract the same kind of ire as a result, slaves in ancient Greece or Rome may have felt similarly insulted by low opinions of their worth as they were compelled to parade up and down a platform before prospective buyers. I know that was how I reacted when, having been made aware of the amount that Rovers wanted, I learned that Widnes had offered a much less.

Talk about differing views! The clubs were nowhere near agreement, someone somewhere was surely taking the Mickey, and I was stuck as a helpless and hapless piggy in the middle. The Rugby Football League, when the issue was referred to tribunal, more or less split the figures down the middle, erring a little towards the Vikings. Even that, though, was full of caveats, with instalments payable over three years and a further amount due if and when I played for Great Britain. It was dispiriting, and my disillusion continued when Widnes pulled out. The snub, which is what I felt it was, came at a bad time for me.

I was still rebuilding my confidence over being rejected by Castleford after a short loan spell at the Jungle, with my Featherstone coach Peter Roe reacting angrily to what he saw as a cavalier attitude to my welfare by the Tigers. Roe—who had been on Yorkshire's coaching staff—had also argued my case, unsuccessfully, for a place in the county squad at the beginning of the summer, when Wigan had been reportedly interested in me. He probably didn't do much for his own future prospects within the Yorkshire camp when he publicly confirmed his disappointment over my omission, declaring that he'd been outvoted. He was forthright, too, when a month-long loan spell at Castleford towards the end of the 2001 season ended in rejection, but I have to admit that I was glad that someone, at what was a difficult time for me, was prepared to stand my corner, and I'll always be grateful to Peter Roe for that.

The Tigers had taken me on a temporary basis for, I think, two reasons. The first was because of an injury to Aussie scrum half Mitch Healy, which made them light at half back, and the second was—I hope—that they wanted to take a good look at me with a view to making a permanent signing. My spell at the Jungle started well enough, if impartial accounts are anything to go by. Although my first match for the Tigers, at Warrington, ended in a 27–12 defeat, I didn't think I had a bad game. Nor did members of the assembled press. I landed four goals and *Rugby Leaguer* reporter Tony Gleave wrote: 'One bright spot for Castleford was the performance of on-loan scrum half Jamie Rooney, who displayed an excellent kicking game and will certainly give coach Graham Steadman some new options for the rest of the season.' Steadman seemed to agree. He said: 'I was very pleased with the contribution of Jamie Rooney, he acquitted himself very well and did everything he was asked to do, and his kicking was outstanding.' In the same paper, Dave 'Nosey' Parker revealed that Huddersfield were hovering in the wings, and I didn't think I did my prospects any harm when Castleford took on Leeds at the Jungle. I was on the bench for this one, a game in which the Tigers lost 17–10 after having been 10–2 up at the interval. One reporter, however, had words of praise, avowing, 'another confident display by Rooney, who came off the bench just as Leeds were getting topside.'

The next game, at Valley Parade against Bradford, turned out to be my last for Castleford, which was surprising to say the least after decent displays in my other two matches. We were unable to contain New Zealand international Henry Paul and were beaten 56–30, and I think it's fair to say that I copped the rap. I hadn't had a good game, I'd be the first to admit that, and I expected my fair share of criticism when we held our team debriefing session early the following week. But I certainly wasn't braced for what was coming. Graham Steadman, speaking to the entire squad, didn't pull his punches when he got around to analysing my performance. He'd made the journey himself, once, from Featherstone to Castleford, as an elusive attacking stand off or full back, and as such maybe I'd expected a bit of empathy, if not understanding.

Instead, I was knocked for six, absolutely flattened, when he announced, in front of the other players, that I wasn't good enough for Super League. And that was it. No mention of his praise for my display at Warrington, no consideration of my good performance against Leeds. Okay, those games had ended in defeat, but I'd played well and given more than a hint of what I could achieve given an extended run. But, on the back of one admittedly indifferent outing, I was to be axed. It was incredible and I still think Steadman should have handled it better. Fair enough, he was the coach and the decision to retain me on loan or even sign me on permanently belonged to him and the board. I can't argue with that. But to tell a lad, in front of others, that he isn't good enough is not impressive, and I don't think I've ever felt so low in a dressing room in my life.

Peter Roe was furious and didn't hold back in his criticisms of Steadman and his condemnation of the Tigers as a whole. The veteran journalist John Robinson covered the issue for the *Rugby Leaguer* and quoted Steadman as saying: 'We have had a good look at Jamie but it is clear that the gulf between Super League and the Northern Ford Premiership is more expansive than we first thought. Working as he does in a part time environment, he would average about 90 hours of training per month. The Tigers do more than that in a week.'

Roe, angry that no one from Castleford had bothered to inform Rovers that I was being returned, retorted:

Cas say that they don't want Jamie yet Graham Steadman has still asked for a private meeting with him. What that will be about, I don't know, and neither does Jamie. But I do know that Jamie has been left in no man's land. The Tigers don't seem to be playing the game, and could have handled this better. If Jamie comes back to Featherstone, and in some ways I hope he does, I will try to pick up his spirits because he is bound to feel low after comments from the Tigers' camp. He is coming out of contract and we have said all along that we will not stand in his way if a Super League club wanted him—and that still applies. He played well against Warrington and Leeds, after which Graham Steadman went to press intimating that the Tigers were looking to do something permanent with him. Unfortunately Jamie did not have his greatest game against Bradford Bulls, so suddenly he was not good enough anymore. It was my recommendation that he went to the Tigers on loan, because he could have held it against us if we had denied him the chance.

Assistant coach Ian Fairhurst backed Roe, saying: 'Jamie is a strong enough character to put this behind him, with a bit of help and guidance from us, and he'll come back stronger for it. The ideal situation now would be for Jamie to help Featherstone Rovers into Super League.'

Somehow, despite my coaches' valued support, I should have known that it wasn't going to be my year. I was picked to play for a Northern Ford Premiership side against a 'Super League Select' team in what was a trial match for the forthcoming England Under 21s tour to South Africa, under John Kear. We won 27–20 and I collected the man of the match award, having a hand in two tries, scoring one myself and kicking the late drop goal that ended a strong rally by the full timers. I felt that, in all the circumstances, I'd done enough to warrant a seat on the plane, but I should have known better in what was turning out to be a strange year in my rugby league career. I wasn't selected.

I didn't delay over re-signing after the Widnes debacle. I have to admit that when the tribunal settled on the amount, I had a little inkling that Widnes wouldn't take me on board, but it was disappointing because that wasn't a lot of money. The Vikings, though, knew more than me what they could afford, and after the setbacks over Yorkshire, Castleford and the Under 21s I decided that I'd just have to roll my sleeves up, keep my head up and get on with my career. There was nothing else I could do; at the end of the day the best place to do my talking was out on the field, with actions rather than words. The philosophy was to stand me in good stead nearly seven years later, when Erika, Brennan and Fletcher were in Germany for Brennan's treatment and things weren't going too well for me at Wakefield Trinity at the beginning of the 2008 campaign. Having struggled with a shoulder injury, I was dropped from the side by coach John Kear and, being 'home alone', had plenty of time to brood over the situation. I do tend to bottle things up a bit too much. It's something I shouldn't do, I know that. It's how I am, and you can't change the way you are, although people might find it surprising that a half back, who appears superficially to be extrovert and outgoing, can tend to be introverted at times.

I set my standards very high, and I was starting to find my feet a little bit and coming to terms with my family not being around. It was difficult, mind, but I knew from experience that just one big performance could lead to me getting my season back on track and that I would, almost inevitably, start playing like I know I can week-in, week-out. In those situations it's a matter of regaining confidence and, above all, of staying positive, although that can be difficult when you're on your own and your family is hundreds of miles away. It was a pretty testing situation and one of the problems, in relation to my rugby, is that when I have an average game it looks as though I'm not playing as well as I can. I know, myself, that it's not that; it's just that I set my standards so high that I want to keep them at that level—if I don't, then I go off the boil.

It can get confusing sometimes over whether a player has had a good game, or a bad game. I know that sounds a bit 'Irish', and many folk will tell you that players know, themselves, whether they've performed well or not. But it's not always as simple as that and I think many players will privately agree that I'm right. I've sometimes been told by coaches, for example, that I've played well and I've thought to myself, 'I didn't', while on other occasions I've come off feeling reasonably pleased with my performance and been told that I'd played poorly. It depends, largely, on what a coach wants from a player. As a half back, my main aim is to go out, get my defence right and set up tries. The coach may simply want me to organise the

side. If I've done that right, the coach will think
I've had a good game, while the fans, unaware of
the instructions, might think I've had a quiet
match and be critical. It can, of course, work the
other way round, when the coach asks a player to
provide some structure but he goes off on his own
agenda with some flashy play which might suit the
supporters but which in reality undermines the
team's whole strategy.

That probably applies more to hookers than to
any other player, including the half backs, where
the direction from dummy half is so crucial these
days. So it's pretty complicated but, having said all
that, I suppose I do know in my own mind when
I've played well and when I haven't. I'm always
looking at things I can improve and I'll continue
to do that until I retire. One of the aspects of being
a half back, of course, is that you're a creator.
Sport, especially a team sport, can often be about
minimising mistakes, even at the highest level.
Everybody's making mistakes out there all the
time; both sets of players, the match officials,
indeed everyone who is involved, either directly
or indirectly. Those whose task it is to make
opportunities for others are in a slightly different
category. For us, whether it's half backs in rugby
league, midfield players in soccer or the spinners
in cricket, it's not so much about cutting down on
errors as coming up with something special to help
the team win a match.

Having said that, hard work does make up for
your mistakes, but you can miss three tackles and
then score a fabulous try and the three tackles

you've missed are all forgotten—by the fans anyway. Not by the coach or the video reviewers, though. At the end of the day we play rugby for ourselves and for our team-mates, but the fans do pay our wages. I'll talk to any of them, I'm not one who gets riled by them shouting abuse at me, I'll just ignore that and get on with it. I know that a couple of weeks down the line I'll be their best mate again, when I've had a good game. It's swings and roundabouts, one week you're up, the next week you're down and it's the same in life really.

As a player, you have to be able to take criticism on the chin. If you can't do that, you're in the wrong job. The supporters pay their hard-earned money to come and watch, and if they want to shout abuse at you, that's up to them. You have to ignore it, and get on with your game. It can be infuriating if you allow it to be; one week, you're the next-best thing since sliced bread, the week after you're rubbish, but it's important that you keep a level head. Some players can deal with it, and others can't. Some players, for reasons best known to themselves, log on to the fans' forums on the internet, and it demoralises them. I read them now and then, I admit, but it has no effect. I just laugh at some of the stuff on there, even when it's praising me, because it can make me wonder what they've been watching.

Not that they're always wrong, but coaches tend to know what they're talking about, in the vast majority of cases anyway. One of the best I've come across was Tony Smith, who did such a good job with Huddersfield Giants and then Leeds—

steering the Rhinos to their first championship in 35 years in 2005—before being appointed coach of Great Britain. Smith picked me for the Northern Union side that took on the All Golds in the Centenary International at the Halliwell Jones Stadium, Warrington, in autumn 2007. It was another occasion that didn't go too well for me, and I couldn't quite put my finger on why. The build-up of being in the camp, alongside the likes of Terry Newton and Adrian Morley, was a weird experience. Like everyone else in the Northern Union side that night, I was determined to make a real impact in the hope that I could force my way belatedly into the Great Britain squad for the forthcoming Test series against New Zealand.

Maybe I tried too hard, but somehow I never quite got going. It was a funny game, I wasn't overawed and I'd been looking forward to the occasion, in fact I'd been building, throughout my entire career, towards that match. But it seemed somehow to be over before it started. Tony Smith sat me down and told me that I wouldn't be in the Great Britain squad for the series. He gave me a few things to work on, but he stressed that the door remained open. It was the first time I'd spoken to him properly; he's straight down the line, and he tells you the areas on which you need to work. He spoke about my defence, and how to deal with being a target for the ball carriers, and about my line running. Until John Kear took over at Wakefield, no one had ever mentioned that to me. He told me, in terms of my tackling, to go low and make my one-on-ones, and in attack to stop running across the field before passing, to halt, and stop the defence from going over to my outside backs.

It was like a weight off my shoulders. My experience of being in the set up will stand me in good stead, and I'll be more relaxed in future, but in another sense it panned out well. The build-up to the Northern Union game was great but now the season was over I was sore and tired. I needed an operation on my shoulder and the fact that I was no longer in the running for the Test Series meant I could get that over and done with well before the 2008 Super League season. I'd also be able to take the family on holiday. I've touched on my own little difficulties during what has, in truth, been a reasonably happy and successful career so far, and of the problems or setbacks endured by David Beckham and Andrew Flintoff and, maybe, Christiano Ronaldo. It's hard to imagine, though, how Dwain Chambers, a bloke who certainly did wrong but as far as I can see has served his punishment, feels in trying to resurrect his career.

Chambers has proved he is a world class sprinter but missed out on the 2008 Olympics in Beijing because of his previous ban for taking drugs. As we all know, he tried to continue to earn a living by turning to rugby league, with Castleford Tigers. As far as I'm concerned, if the bloke wanted to have a crack, fair enough. He is a sprinter at the end of the day and playing rugby league is a world away from running down a 100-metre sprint track with flimsy footwear on. Plus he'd got 18 stone props running after him, that was always likely to be a bit of a chase. His flirtation with rugby league certainly attracted huge publicity and opinion was divided over whether it was for the better or for the worse. I didn't, in truth, expect much to come of it. It's sad that no one will touch him in athletics now; maybe they should, after all he's done his time, as far as I can see. But he was always going to struggle, far more than the likes of Berwyn Jones, with Wakefield in the 1960s, and Alf Meakin who signed for Leeds at around the same time. It's not like the old days when wingers regularly had overlaps; sliding defences have cut down on those opportunities, they would just have had to kick for him and let him gallop. But then he'd have to pick the ball up.

I'd liked to have seen him play in the trial game against York City Knights, it sounded as though it was a bit of an occasion, and it certainly interested everybody. But he wanted £60,000 a year at the Jungle and he seemed to be saying it as if it was nothing. I suspect that all those lads at Cas were thinking, 'Who does he think he is, he's never played and he wants £60,000 a year? Here's the ball then.' He said he could earn that in nine seconds as an athlete, although that's nine seconds built on a lot of training admittedly. But it won't have gone down well with the rugby lads.

7

TUG OF WAR

It was good to get back to Featherstone Rovers after the humiliation heaped on me at Castleford by Graham Steadman. Post Office Road, particularly with the ever-supportive Peter Roe at the helm, was exactly the stage on which I would be able to lick my wounds, regain my dented confidence and composure, and recover—but I was more determined than ever to prove my worth in Super League.

Ideally that would be with Rovers, the team I had supported as a boy and the club which had, after my junior days with Travellers Saints, nurtured and developed me. But the simple truth was that if Featherstone Rovers were to turn out to be, for whatever reason, unable to make it into the top flight, I'd have no alternative other than to move on to pastures new. It wasn't something I particularly wanted. I was happy at Post Office Road, and it wasn't Featherstone's fault that we'd have to part company. But there didn't, at the time, appear to be any place for them in Super League and even now, the best part of a decade down the line, Rovers remain on the outside looking in. It's for others to comment on the rights and the wrongs of that, but from my own personal and possibly selfish perspective, there was a danger of time running out on my ambitions and high expectations for myself.

A sportsman's shelf life is relatively short, there's no doubt about that, and you never know what may be around the corner to shorten it even more. Injuries weren't at the front of my mind, of course, but the possibility of a career-ending knock is probably rooted in any sportsman's subconscious. No rugby league player can go into games thinking too much about what could go wrong; that would be debilitating and could possibly even lead to injuries, through hanging back. For all that, though, we play each game in the full knowledge that in a single split second one bad injury can end a promising or high-flying career. I was also conscious, or at least half-aware, that players in the Northern Ford Premiership—now the Co-operative Championships—can perhaps be more at risk than those in Super League. That's not necessarily because the rugby is harder as such, nor is it because the players are tougher, or even less disposed to high standards of discipline. But in my opinion the fact that so many games in Super League are televised, and played under the relentless spotlight of a plethora of cameras, makes it difficult for those who are tempted to inflict any off-the-ball damage to get away with it scot-free. Because of that, I think that there is definitely more 'self policing' in the top flight of the professional game, and that extra degree of control can only help the ball players, the artists and the players whom the fans pay to see more than anyone, in their hopes for lengthy and prosperous careers.

Not that the impression should be given in any way that rugby league outside Super League is an arena for thugs or hatchet men; the blokes whose aim is to put an opposing player out of the game. It isn't. Coaches at all levels, including those in the amateur game and particularly in the well-run National Conference League, tend to work very much to a percentage system these days, with spread sheets, DVDs and other modern tools of the trade enabling them to analyse every aspect of play, both by their own teams and by the opposition. All coaches seem to work to the same principles and, to a man, they won't be happy if sets are not completed, for example, or if their team ends up on the wrong end of the penalty count. Nor are they enthusiastic about missed tackles— no change there from the old days—which are ticked off with relentless efficiency by the statisticians on the sidelines. A key factor, though, is the penalty count—not to mention the loss of a player through a yellow card for a sin binning or a red card for a permanent dismissal—and because of that more than anything else it's fair to say that the old-style 'hatchet man' is now a rarity, if he exists at all. All the same, though, the existence of so many cameras at Super League matches is an extra and welcome deterrent against the odd descent of the red mist. And that makes the top flight of the domestic game a much better vehicle for half backs such as me to parade our skills.

Not that I had too many problems at Featherstone, to be fair, and I certainly began to enjoy myself again on my return to action in the famous irregular blue and white hoops. Fixtures outside the top tier commenced before Christmas at that time, in a bid to boost attendances I think, and December 2001 opened with a game at Chorley, where I helped Rovers to a 21–2 half time lead against nuggety opposition before we closed with a reasonably hard-earned 28–16 victory. We weren't so thrilled seven days later, when we let a 17–10 lead wither way in an 18–17 defeat by Workington Town. That was a stunner of a defeat and not one we were too happy about as the Cumbrians had not prevailed at Post Office Road for 47 years, their last win on our ground having been registered only a couple of seasons after Town had beaten Featherstone at Wembley.

It was close, too, at Gateshead, where I had to remain calm and collected in converting a try three minutes from time which enabled us, after a testing and difficult game, to escape with a 12–12 draw against an improving north eastern outfit that, in 2000, had taken 19 games to get off the mark. But my own form was okay, I was gradually but steadily getting my confidence back after the dispiriting Steadman slight, and I had a nice Yuletide present when the papers reported, on Christmas Eve, that Peter Roe—now the coach at Wakefield Trinity—had confirmed that he wanted me to join him at Belle Vue. The Wildcats, unfortunately, were seriously cash-strapped at the time. It may have been during the period when

John Pearman, a freeman of the city, seemed to go off the rails. He made a series of promises which, it was subsequently found, had little or no substance and caused Wakefield Trinity to amass some serious debts. Whether that was the underlying problem or not I don't know, but chairman Ted Richardson was unable, despite his best efforts, to produce the £40,000 to secure my transfer from Post Office Road. For the moment I was quite happy to continue plying my trade in a Featherstone Rovers shirt, although it wasn't all plain sailing by any means.

We were certainly giving our loyal legion of supporters value for money, at least in terms of edge-of-the-seat excitement, and we came close to snatching a remarkable victory against Huddersfield in the very first fixture of the New Year. The Giants, playing impressively, were 21–8 ahead with only six minutes left but we came up with the goods when it mattered. I raised our hopes when I sent Jamie Stokes over and improved his score, and the match was suddenly very much in the balance when I again added the conversion after Stokes notched a second touchdown in double-quick time. That goal put us a mere point adrift, but for once I was unable to rescue the side at the death, my long range drop goal attempt in the closing seconds drifting agonisingly wide of the posts.

It went better for us at Keighley a few weeks later, though. Keith Reeves was the rugby leaguer's man at Cougar Park but he's no one-eyed journo. He's a bloke who knows the game through and through and is always happy to delight in impressive performances by the visitors. Reeves wrote of our 36–16 win:

> Keighley led 16–10 at the break and must have been optimistic of going on to secure the points. But Jamie Rooney had other ideas. He put on a near-perfect, near precision kicking display in the second half to lead his team to victory. He landed seven second half goals, four penalties including a towering effort from the half way line, and added all three conversions to Rovers' second half tries. His influence didn't end there. He created two tries for Martin Shaw and added a try of his own, the final score five minutes from time when he hacked ahead after a Keighley error near half way. Naturally he added the conversion, for a personal 20-point haul.

Shaw's first try gave me particular pleasure, coming as it did from a 70-metre, 40/20 kick, and I was delighted to help us to a sixth win in seven games when we beat Hull Kingston Rovers 43–12. I scored a try in the second minute, added seven goals, including three from the touchline, and landed a drop goal, while I celebrated my 22nd birthday in mid-March with 32 points from four tries and eight goals in a 64–6 stroll over Swinton.

By early April I'd passed the 1,000 point mark in my career. I broke the barrier at Gateshead, where my 20 points from a try and 11 goals in the

56–6 win took me to 1,009 points in 98 matches. By this stage, Super League clubs were hovering again, but I'd become a shade wary after my experiences of the previous year or two. My preference was that I'd move into the top flight with my hometown club, Featherstone Rovers—a message I repeatedly gave to journalists.

Erika, meanwhile, was pregnant, which was fantastic news, although any prospective dad will, I'm sure, agree that the pending arrival focuses your mind on many issues, including the financial aspect. So the inevitable happened. Brennan was born in October 2002, on the evening I was at the Northern Ford Premiership Awards Dinner at Elland Road with Featherstone, and a month or two later, with Rovers having missed out on promotion, I joined Wakefield Trinity Wildcats. A 'Getting to Know' feature in *League Express* in December 2002 is, with hindsight, revealing. Alongside the usual confidences, such as boyhood heroes—Deryck Fox and Brendan Tuuta—I revealed that we'd just had a baby and told of how, when I'd gone to the NFP dinner, I'd given Erika clear instructions not to give birth that night. I told the *Express*: 'But I got a call when I was there telling me she'd gone into labour nine weeks early. Brennan is fine now, he's at home with us.'

He wasn't fine of course, which was something we didn't know—but certainly suspected—at the time. I, for my part, **was** fine, if a little disorientated at being at Belle Vue after more than six years at Post Office Road, where I'd pretty much come of age in rugby league terms. One thing is for sure, and there's no point denying it. The 10-year-old Jamie Rooney would never have contemplated playing for Wakefield Trinity, or for any other professional club, for that matter. That young lad only wanted to play for Featherstone Rovers, who were in the top flight, the old First Division, at the time. When I watched them from the terraces as an enthralled and highly vocal young fan they were playing the likes of Leeds, Wigan and St Helens, and often beating them. When I finally put pen to paper at Post Office Road, I imagined that that was it, and that I'd never leave. It was, for me at the time, a lifetime commitment. When I gravitated to the first team, and started to pick up a few man of the match awards, I grew to like it even more and seriously believed that I'd be at the Rovers for the rest of my career. I'm happy to say that now I'm thinking exactly the same about Wakefield.

It was a wrench leaving Featherstone. I'm a Featherstone lad, after all, and had only ever played locally, first for Travellers, and at school, then with Rovers. In fact I don't mind admitting that it was difficult. I'd grown up in Featherstone, I still lived there and Rovers had always been my team. But at the end of the day I knew Rovers would probably never be in Super League, which is a crying shame because I'd have liked to play in that competition with Featherstone. It just came about that Wakefield Trinity Wildcats were interested. They were a local side, and we'd just had Brennan, so it was the perfect club for us, just up the road and handy.

Above all, I wanted to play Super League. Leaving Featherstone was difficult but to this day, for all my initial anguish, I don't regret going at the time that I did. I'm playing in the major arena, which was something I'd always dreamed about, and I want to carry on doing that for as long as I can, even though I wouldn't mind ending my career at Post Office Road. Rovers have a long history of talented players moving on, in fact that's how they've kept going over the years. Most have left with the perception of wanting to better themselves, which is a view that very often could have been argued about, particularly when all the clubs were in one league; and even in the days of two divisions, when Featherstone were as often as not in the top tier. In my case, however, there was clearly no alternative. I was in two minds, but at the end of the day the move to Wakefield Trinity Wildcats meant having a full time job. I was paid a lot more money than I received at Featherstone. That isn't always the most important thing but the reality was that I'd just had a little lad, and Erika and I had to start looking after him. I was still living at home with my mum at the time, and I needed to get a house for my family. Everything just seemed to happen in that one year. The baby arrived, we needed our own home and I got a new contract with Wakefield.

So the timing of it all was, in that sense, perfect, even if I would have liked to have played Super League earlier in my career; but these things happen, and maybe the sequence of events benefited me in a way. I played first team rugby for quite a while at Post Office Road, serving my initial apprenticeship in effect. As it panned out, I had a few months in the Under 21s at Belle Vue before going into the first team, which I suppose completed the learning process as a young player—although, as anyone will tell you, you never stop learning in this game. When I finally played for the Wildcats first team I became one of only a few men to have played at each of the famous three of Featherstone Rovers, Wakefield Trinity Wildcats and Castleford Tigers. I believe only a handful have accomplished that and after seven years now at Trinity I certainly owe a lot to the Wildcats, as well as to Rovers, for providing me with a career in which I'm doing something I enjoy so much.

While Featherstone and Wakefield are obviously rivals, and have been for a long time, the real animosity between the fans seems to be limited to Rovers and Castleford supporters. It's still classed as a local 'derby', though, when the Wildcats and Featherstone meet, so quite a few comments were made at the time I switched. I really do think that most people understood and accepted my reasons behind the switch, particularly those who had known me for some time as a person. They appreciated that I had to further my career, just as I would do in any other walk of life. I obviously get a bit of stick from some people who feel, to this day, that I shouldn't have left Rovers, but I honestly think that deep down they, too, also understand why I did it. It was a little bit about money, yes, but fundamentally I just wanted to better my career. The only way I was going to do that was if I was going to go full time, alongside other full time players and under full time coaches, and I don't think anyone can begrudge me doing that.

I always found Featherstone Rovers fans to be superb, as passionate and well-informed—and supportive—as any in the game. I can say the same about their equivalents at Wakefield Trinity Wildcats, where a group of supporters have banded together as the Wakefield Independent Supporters Club Association (WISCA) and have raised many tens of thousands of pounds for the parent club towards team-building and other projects. Shortly after signing for Wakefield, I was back at Post Office Road again—this time in a Trinity shirt. To come straight back to my roots, for a Boxing Day friendly, was memorable and I think I was probably more nervous and keyed up for that game than I've ever been in a rugby league match in all my life. To break all the records at a club, especially the one you followed fervently as a lad, and then to come back in the opposing side was pretty nerve racking. I got a bit of rhubarb off the fans and from the players as well, which was to be expected. It was just a bit of friendly banter really, and I'm sure it will continue whenever we play Featherstone Rovers.

I've already referred to Featherstone's great traditions, and I was very conscious that, in moving to Wakefield Trinity Wildcats, I was joining a club with an equally illustrious history. Many Trinity fans will, indeed, insist that they have achieved even more than Rovers over the years, and I suppose the fact that they are one of the oldest clubs in the game, having been launched in 1873, has inevitably helped them gain an 'edge' in terms of trophies won. While Rovers have something unique in their wonderful irregular blue and white hooped jerseys, Wakefield are also special in their choice of name; by which I mean 'Trinity', 'Wildcats' having been added on the launch of Super League in 1996.

The soubriquet has, as you might suspect, religious connotations, Wakefield Trinity having been formed by members of a young men's society at the nearby Holy Trinity Church. Early matches were played just up the road, on Heath Common, which I don't think will have changed much in the intervening years, and the first game at Belle Vue was played in 1879, against a team called Birch. Trinity, as a rugby union club, won the Yorkshire Cup that very year, which was an astonishing achievement when you think about it, and the club emulated that success in 1880, 1883 and 1887, finishing as runners-up on five other occasions.

Wakefield Trinity were clearly a real power in their early days. It wasn't surprising that they were among the 22 clubs that formed the Northern Union in 1895 over the issue of 'broken time' payments for working lads who otherwise could hardly afford to take time off work to play a sport dominated in the south of England by public schools and the like. Trinity started slowly in the Northern Union (which, in the 1920s, was renamed rugby league in deference to Australian sensibilities). The side played in Division Two in the early years, not particularly pulling up any pots, but reached their first Challenge Cup Final in 1909, beating Hull before losing to the same opponents in the 1914 decider.

Wakefield also won the Yorkshire Cup, a major competition in those days, before the First World War, in 1910–11, when they also topped the Yorkshire League, which had first been secured the previous season. Apart from a Yorkshire Cup success in 1924–25—and the presence of the great Jonty Parkin in the 1920s—Trinity tended to be among the also-rans until the end of the Second World War. Wakefield, however, put those decades of sustained disappointment behind them with immediate effect, winning the 1946 Challenge Cup Final at Wembley in what became known as Billy Stott's final, our captain and centre clinching the game against Wigan with a sensational penalty in the last minute landed from five yards inside his own half.

Trinity had to wait a while before returning to the Twin Towers. The arrival of coach Ken Traill from Bradford Northern, and the capture of great players such as centre Neil Fox, tough-as-teak loose forward Derek 'Rocky' Turner, stand off Harold Poynton and South African centre Alan Skene, sent the club on the pathway to real and continued glory in the 1960s. Wakefield appeared in four Challenge Cup Finals during a glittering decade, winning three of them and missing out on just one as they became one of the glamour clubs of rugby league. Hull were beaten 38–5 in 1960,

Fox scoring two tries and six goals, with Skene and scrum half Keith Holliday bagging a brace apiece and stand off Ken Rollin and winger Fred Smith adding touchdowns. Trinity, who were runners-up in the championship, would probably have won in any case against a team that finished third but seven points adrift, but their cause was certainly helped by an injury crisis at the Boulevard of such severity that young second row Mike Smith was called up for his first team debut at Wembley of all places. You wouldn't dare make that up and there is another 'storybook' angle to the final when, despite the margin of victory, journalists voted Hull hooker Tommy Harris, who played with concussion, refusing to come off in the days before substitutes, the Lance Todd Trophy winner as man of the match.

Wakefield were back at the national stadium two years later, and on this occasion Trinity were firmly on course for the fabulous All Four Cups feat. Traill had already secured the Yorkshire Cup and the Yorkshire League, and their opponents in the Challenge Cup Final—Huddersfield—would also provide the opposition seven days later in the Championship Final. Wakefield surmounted the penultimate hurdle against a side that had themselves won All Four Cups in 1914–15, thanks largely to Neil Fox, who landed three drop goals— worth two points each at that time—and, with winger Ken Hirst, scored a try in the 12–6 win and took the Lance Todd Trophy in recognition of his achievement.

The only disappointed bloke in the Trinity camp

that day, I would imagine, was prop Don Vines, whose knee injury ultimately prevented him from making a record fourth successive appearance at Wembley. He had previously played for Wakefield in the 1960 final and for St Helens a year later, with another outing due with Trinity (although he didn't know it at the time of course) in 1963. Another upset character that springtime afternoon was Huddersfield's classy scrum half and captain Tommy Smales, who was later to become such an important figure in my life. Tommy gained revenge the following Saturday, when Fartown shattered Trinity's hopes of joining the immortals with a 14–5 victory in the Championship Final at Odsal, Bradford. Wakefield, however, quickly recovered and retained the Challenge Cup 12 months later when, with the Yugoslavian Milan Kosanovic at hooker and 20-year-old Ian Brooke partnering Neil Fox in the centre, Wigan were beaten 25–10, Poynton picking up the Lance Todd Trophy for a typically majestic display. South African winger Gert Coetzer scored two tries in the win, with prop Malcolm Sampson, Poynton and Brooke also touching down and Neil Fox landing five goals.

Trinity had been a trifle lucky again on the injury front that afternoon as Wigan suffered through an injury to full back David Bolton who sustained concussion but opted to return to the fray. His wife, who rushed to the dressing rooms after the match to check on his condition, was given a real scare when a couple of ambulance men told her, for whatever reason, that he was dead!

Dame Fortune wasn't on Wakefield's side in the 1968 final. This was the famous game that shouldn't have gone ahead, one that has entered the annals of not only rugby league but sporting folklore. Torrential rain flooded the pitch an hour or so before the kick off but referee J.P. Hebblethwaite of York felt he had no alternative other than to give the nod for the match to be played, simply because tens of thousands of supporters had travelled down from the north for the occasion.

The 87,100 crowd, and millions of television viewers, witnessed a memorable spectacle that barely qualified as sport. It was more drama, pure theatre—veering very often on farce—with a number of players saying later that they had been in danger of drowning when tackled. With Neil Fox sidelined through injury his brother Don—another of rugby league's 'greats'—took on the kicking duties. Opponents Leeds appeared to have snatched victory with a late penalty try by Great Britain winger John Atkinson, his Great Britain colleague, full back Bev Risman, adding the conversion and, two minutes from time, a long range penalty to establish an 11–7 lead. In a sensational finish, though, Don Fox's clever kick-off gave Ken Hirst a glimmer of a chance, the winger hacking on a couple of times in defiance of desperate defenders to pounce on the ball at the side of the posts.

In those days a try was worth only three points and it therefore fell to Fox, who had already converted Hirst's first half try in addition to having landed a penalty, to slot over the winning goal. It was plain sailing, surely. But in dreadful conditions that really were more suited to sailing than to rugby Fox sliced his kick wide before collapsing in disbelief and despair on the Wembley turf, BBC TV commentator Eddie Waring proclaiming, 'Poor lad!' in one of the most memorable moments in sporting history while the tannoy operator announced that Fox had already been selected as the Lance Todd Trophy winner. Wakefield, who had won the championship for the first time the previous season, beating St Helens in the final after a replay, retained the title to gain some solace for that defeat but, in those days, the Challenge Cup was practically the be-all and end-all.

Trinity had to wait for over a decade to return to Wembley, stand off David Topliss helping inspire a superb semi-final win over St Helens with a memorable break that led to winger Andy Fletcher grabbing a late winner at Headingley. Widnes had the better of a dour affair in the decider, grinding out a 12–3 victory in which Wakefield's only consolation was the fact that Topliss won the Lance Todd Trophy. Wakefield haven't quite been able to hit the heights since, although they won the Yorkshire Cup in 1992–93 and Trinity are now, I think, the permanent holders as that was the last occasion, when Sheffield Eagles were disposed of, that the competition was held.

Under John Kear there is now a definite, tangible feeling that the good times may be about to return, although it wasn't quite like that at all when I arrived at Belle Vue, in fact the state of the place came as a real shock to me. It was stunning, to be frank. The Wildcats, I discovered to my dismay, didn't have a conditioner, and there was no training gear. I wondered what the hell I'd come into, although I also thought that maybe it was normal for Super League. It was all new to me, but after I'd been to dressing rooms at away games I'd return to Wakefield and think to myself, 'What's this we've got at Belle Vue, a shed?'

Thankfully John Kear's hard work has transformed all that, and the signs are that we could be on our way back to reviving former glories, although there's obviously quite a way to go yet in that regard. We're often described as a sleeping giant, as one of the greatest clubs in the sport, and I'm fully aware of Wakefield Trinity's history and of the superb players who have graced Belle Vue for the past century and a half or so. Several former stalwarts still visit the club on a regular basis, including ex-players such as Neil Fox. David Topliss, before his tragic death, often popped in, and I look up to them. We all do in fact. I see Neil quite a lot at Belle Vue, doing a bit of exercising on the bike or having a lie down in the sauna, and I still sometimes think, 'I'm sitting here talking to Neil Fox, it's unbelievable,' and pinch myself. I found my voice catching the first couple of times I met him but he's more like a mate now. People like that, who played at Wakefield for so long and who just want the best for the club after they've finished, deserve a massive amount of credit. You get some players who finish their careers and who then proceed to write the game off, but Neil's not one of those, and neither was David Topliss. Both of them shared the same philosophy—they and others such as Ian Brooke want (wanted, sadly, in David's case) to help rugby league and to do what they can for Wakefield.

Neil Fox talks about the game a great deal but he doesn't go into too much detail; he's always constructive and he's not the type of bloke to start criticising players. He's just a nice fella, and there are a lot of them around at Wakefield. Shane McNally and Adrian Vowles were also good blokes and I was lucky that they were my coaches in my first few seasons at Belle Vue, not that it always felt that way at the time. They looked after me, as a young and ambitious player about to make his mark in Super League. McNally, my first boss at Wakefield Trinity Wildcats, nursed me through. He'd play me a few times, then rest me, because he didn't want me to get too far ahead of myself. I wasn't pleased, I've got to admit. At the time I thought, 'I'm ready, I'm ready. Play me.' But looking back I think it was the right thing to do on Shane and Peter's part.

I'd come from being the standout player at Featherstone Rovers, in the National League, directly to Super League, where there are many players around of a similar calibre. The main difference, for me, was the physical strength of the players, both in our own ranks and in the opposition, and that stood out immediately. It's a lot easier to get fit when you're full time, able to focus on weight training and suchlike through the day, than when you're working, and training at night. When I first came to Wakefield I picked up quite a few injuries—you expect that as a half back, you can be targeted by the opposition runners but the Gareth Ellis's of this world just love tackling and will go out of their way to tackle players for you. That makes your job a lot easier. Some players just love to tackle and we've got a few of those at the Wildcats now. Kevin Henderson will defend all day, to have him inside you and Jason Demetriou outside is a massive help. Players will hesitate to run at you too often because with those two alongside they know they're going to get bashed, and that there will be a third or fourth man coming in to kill them as well. Your team-mates want you, as a half back, to be fresh in attack, so they tend to be happy to cover for you. But you're much better equipped to do your own stint when you've been training full time, including spending plenty of time on the weights.

It was a bit strange in my early days at Belle Vue, and never more so than during the period when I was being nursed along. When I first arrived at Wakefield I'd just got the Player of the Year award at Featherstone Rovers, and I'd been voted the National League Young Player of the Year. I came to Trinity and, as part of my gradual introduction, was picked for the Wildcats' Under 21s team against Rovers Under 21s at Post Office Road. That was a weird situation, having played for the first team at Featherstone and then coming back at Under 21s; in fact it was difficult.

Wakefield's first team wasn't doing that well and I thought, 'Surely I must get my chance this time', but it was about half way through the season before Shane McNally gave me my opportunity. Looking back now, I think he was right in what he did, nursing me through into the first team, because it's a lot different in Super League. At the time, I wanted to play, and I couldn't get my head around it, but coaches have been there before with kids. They know what to do, and you've got to respect them for that. It was the same with John Kear. Coaches are not daft blokes, they are coaches for a reason, and in my experience they know what they are doing. At the time though, when Shane McNally wasn't picking me, I have to confess that I couldn't stand the bloke. It was doing my head in that much. But reflecting on it now, it was probably the right decision. He'd explained it to me, telling me that he didn't want to push me in at the deep end, into a losing side, but I'd struggled to accept it. I thought, 'Just give me a chance', but he was right.

In the end I made my debut at Widnes on 25 April 2003, as a substitute, and made my full debut at Leeds, kicking a goal in a one-point defeat. We won at St Helens the following week, and I was selected as the Gamestar seven days later following a win at Halifax, which was the first time that year that we'd had back-to-back wins. Shane McNally had proved his point, he'd put me in the side at the right time and had made the right decision. I grew to like him—he was my first coach in a full time environment—and I learned a lot from him. He fully deserved the recognition when he picked up a Super League Coach of the Year award, and he had a great colleague in Adrian Vowles. They were the first men to give me my chance in Super League, and I owe them a lot for that at a time when others simply didn't want to know. Coaches elsewhere either didn't seem to rate me or thought I wasn't worth the valuation that Rovers had put on my head. At the time I thought I'd never get out of Featherstone.

While all this was going on Erika and I were having a real tug of war with the hospital over Brennan. As soon as it was established that he was poorly, the medical people made it clear that they wanted to tube-feed him. We said no to this, and it's continued to be a very big issue until recently. Our view was that if he doesn't eat—which in some cases the child doesn't, if he is fed through a tube—he'd never learn to speak, because he'd never use the muscles in his mouth. So we argued against that, and refused permission. Brennan started eating and talking, and progressing well, but the consultants at Pontefract continued to insist that he would never walk or talk, or even recognise us.

He's stringing quite a few words together now and continually progressing, but the paediatricians had initially maintained that we should just accept him as he was. Then, when the National Health physiotherapists started to visit us, we were told that certain exercises could improve movement by reducing his muscle tone. That was a big step forward for us, whereas when we saw the doctors at the hospital the reaction was—and, sadly, has remained—negative. The physios, and the people who deal with Brennan's sight, tended to be more positive and they were always willing to offer a bit of hope, which is so important. Erika and I need that to help keep us going.

We've looked at different centres in this country for help, with Brainwaves in Somerset being particularly good, but it gets to Erika, especially, when the hospital adopts a negative stance. That goes right back to the very first conversation we had, when I turned back from Hull on the day they confirmed Brennan's condition to her. When we told them about Advance, another centre we'd heard about, the physios suggested we stick to their programme, they didn't want us to go anywhere else and stuck to their guns about it. Advance, in Grinstead in London, was the first clinic we took Brennan to, about six months after first going on the internet in our quest for more information and someone who could help us and our oldest son. We went there for three years, for week-long sessions, in an effort to open up his capillaries and improve the blood supply to his muscles. The hospital was never happy about us trying these things. They wanted us to stick with what they were telling us to do. When we felt that the treatment at Advance was no longer right for Brennan and decided to stop going, they told us he'd have made that progress anyway, that we'd wasted a lot of money going there. We were made to feel that we were never doing the right thing.

But we don't regret going, and are not sorry about any of the things we've done. In the end, you have to go with your instincts.

Brainwaves were good, much friendlier than Advance in truth. They were excellent at the little things, for example they'd give Brennan certificates, which were a nice touch, and they made us all feel extra welcome. The man at Brainwaves was very supportive of Brennan and very friendly, whereas it's never been the same at the hospital. One thing that was very good about Brainwaves was that they never promised anything. They just said, 'We'll try, and we'll do our best,' and that kept us going. We wanted to keep it up, too, partly because they were setting targets; when we went back we felt as though we were hitting goals.

They were interested as people, which is something we didn't find when we went back to the hospital. We'd tell them, for example, that Brennan was speaking five more words and they'd pretty much ignore that and say, 'Yes, but he's not eating'. Their focus on the need for tube feeding has always been a worry. The tube would go straight through into his stomach, into the gut, and he would be fed at night. The tube would be attached to a tap into which food is fed, via a syringe. They insisted that they'd top him up during the night with enough calories to ensure that he'd gain weight. The centres we've been to have responded that once you start feeding straight into the gut, children are full during the night and therefore lose interest in food during the day, so the end result is that they don't gain any weight. Brennan, in fact, hasn't put on any weight since he was four, but he's grown, and he's healthy.

We ended up spinning around, and it's been hard to know what to do for the best, but our big worry about Bren being fed through his stomach was that it could affect his speech. It's been a serious issue. Erika went to our GP about it, and he advised against it. In his opinion tube feeding would make Brennan more disabled. The hospital stuck to their guns leaving us continually in limbo. Their argument was that because Brennan has constant spasms, and because he has to exercise all the time, he uses too many calories—that whatever he is fed through his mouth will never be enough, because of all the energy he uses. They really pushed us to do it. According to them, we would be amazed by the progress that could be made just by giving him extra calories. It felt like we were being blackmailed. The hospital knew how much we wanted him to sit up, so they pressed the point that he should have the tube. We didn't know what to do.

We'd have liked them to just sit down and ask us how we felt about it, but they didn't. Every time we went, there was a big argument for 20 minutes and everybody became irate. The consultant said, in front of Erika and her mother, that she didn't feel she would be doing her job properly as a doctor if she didn't try to get us to tube feed Brennan, and that we needed to think about him, not about ourselves. That was distressing. Brennan was just a patient to her—if she had a better manner, we might have listened to her, but it was often difficult. Erika told her, in no uncertain terms, that all we've ever thought about is Brennan, and that of course we want the best for him. But we don't know what that 'best' is, because of all the conflicting advice. If we knew, for certain, that the tube was the best thing, we'd have done that. But we don't know.

Once it's in that's it. He'd have to have an operation to take it out, so the matter would be out of our hands then, which is our big concern. For example, we've put Brennan on medicines before, which we've been doubtful about, and we've been able to take him off them ourselves; we've had some control. But with a tube, once it's in, only the hospital would be able to take it out. We'd have to ask them and they wouldn't be obliged to do it. That kind of decision is a big one, and it isn't one we wanted to rush into, but on the other hand we needed to do something quickly.

Erika wasn't impressed by the sight of children at the Advance centre who had food pumped into their stomachs and who vomited it back immediately. Quite a few people there had tried tube feeding—it hadn't worked, so they'd had the tubes taken out. There were others it had worked for, to be fair, but Erika was put off by those for whom it failed.

Meanwhile Georgia, the little girl from London, went to the centre in Germany a couple of years ago, and she's walking now. So everything pointed to us taking Brennan to the TheraSuitReha Centre in Ratingen. The experts tell us how to bring up our kids. They know a lot technically, I don't dispute that, but they don't necessarily know what's best for each individual child.

Not that it's always clear cut dealing with a rugby player's injuries. I broke my ankle at Castleford in 2004 (David Wrench sustained an identical injury in the same game). I slipped, after breaking ribs a couple of weeks earlier. The hospital said my ankle wasn't broken, but it was. I'd taken painkillers for my ribs, so I didn't feel as much pain from my ankle as I should have done. In fact I thought I'd hurt my knee and I tried to 'run' it off. That injury caused me to miss the play-offs, which was a blow—while another setback at Wakefield was the occasion on which Tony 'Casper' Smith, who had taken over after Shane McNally got the sack, dropped me. Smith also took my number 6 shirt from me and gave me number 16, which isn't what any stand off wants. Generally, though, I've had a good time at Wakefield, and I can't see that I'd rather be at any other Super League club.

There was a possibility, at one time, of a move to London. I hope Harlequins become a real power in the game, because it does no harm at all having a strong presence in the capital. I know there's a strong youth and junior infrastructure in London, but you'd think, with the size of the population, that Harlequins would get 50,000 crowds. Having said that, it's a good job they don't, because they'd be streets ahead of everyone else otherwise. The trouble is that there are so many football teams in the capital, and rugby union is a big sport down there. Rugby league is bottom of the pile and there seems to be an instant perception, when thinking of Harlequins, of a dead-end club.

That's unfair, though. When we were nearly relegated the other year, I spoke to the Broncos, as Harlequins were then called, and they were interested in me. I spoke to them because I wasn't sure what was going to happen, but I was praying that Wakefield would stay up because I didn't fancy moving the family to London. As a single bloke, or even as a childless couple, you'd jump at the chance, but it's a different matter when you have a couple of kids. It's not fair on them; and Brennan's condition means he needs to be around his wider family more than most children.

That played a big part in my decision. To be fair to London, they were superb and offered to pay for his treatment while we were down there. But family is very important and that's the overriding reason I've stayed local. I've had chances to move over the Pennines, in some instances for a lot more money than I get at Wakefield Trinity Wildcats, but in the final analysis family has to come before money.

8

THE GREAT ESCAPE

When John Kear was appointed coach at Belle Vue in late July 2006, Wakefield Trinity Wildcats were, unquestionably, an odds-on bet for relegation. The side, under Tony 'Casper' Smith, were languishing at the foot of the Super League table. On any sensible analysis there was very little hope, if any, of survival. What happened next was remarkable, one of the most amazing escape acts in Super League history. In fact, it's hard to think of any that can come close to matching it.

Kear, who had been booted out at Hull FC—I occasionally wonder if the folk in charge of matters at the KC Stadium sometimes reflect on the wisdom or otherwise of that act—weaved a magic spell. He steered us through a series of gutsy wins and brought the whole adventure to a stunning climax with a vital and dramatic victory over our neighbours Castleford that secured our berth in the top flight for the following season. On Saturday 16 September 2006 a crowd of 11,000 packed into Belle Vue to witness one of the most important fixtures ever played between Wakefield Trinity and Castleford since the clubs first locked horns in the latter's debut season in the Rugby Football League in the 1926–27 campaign 80 years earlier. The Wildcats had already beaten the Tigers twice in the league during the 2006 season, helping to set the scene for one of the most astonishing survival bids in the history of sport, never mind in rugby league.

The headlines said it all after Wakefield Trinity Wildcats mounted a stunning 29–17 victory to leapfrog Castleford Tigers in the last match of the season and send their old rivals tumbling down into National League One. 'Saviour Kear' screamed the front page of *League Weekly* adding, 'Hallelujah! Trinity come back from the dead' and the paper was right to heap praise on our coach, who ironically had been born and raised in Wheldon Road, the home of the Tigers. John Kear had pulled on his vast knowledge of the game to work a major miracle in guiding us to safety, somehow inspiring a side that had lost 16 of its previous 22 league games, many by convincing margins, to winning, dramatically, four of its last six.

The achievement confirmed his abilities only a few short months after he had been sacked by Hull FC, whom he had led to Challenge Cup glory less than a year earlier. I was delighted to make a positive contribution, having something of an impact by kicking four goals and, 12 minutes from time, landing the drop goal that helped establish a seven-point lead. Fortune favours the brave, they reckon, and we had a stroke of luck when my 'bomb', straight from a scrum, was allowed to bounce by Tigers winger Luke Dyer, the Aussie paying a high price when our centre James Evans grabbed the clinching touchdown. I had to feel sorry for Dyer, who had a miserable night under repeated pressure from my kicks. But not too sorry. We owed our survival, as much as anything, to sheer guts in battling back from an early 11–2 deficit after I'd opened the scoring with an early penalty, the match itself mirroring our ascent from the dead in the season itself. Kear, the consummate professional, won't have had mixed feelings about the result, but part of him—maybe the five-year-old boy who, hot water bottle stuffed up his jumper, used to man the scoreboard at Castleford in the 1960s—had natural sympathy for the Tigers. He said:

> I'm very tired and emotional, but it's been a great two months. The players have responded magnificently; they just kept getting better and better on the practice pitch and that's shown in how they've performed on game day. I'm delighted for them, the supporters, the board of directors, Ted Richardson, Steve Ferres—they've all worked and backed us to the hilt and we've paid them back. It's just a marvellous night to avoid relegation—I feel desperately sorry for Castleford coach Terry Matterson, who I think has done a great job, but those were the rules beforehand and people will have to question the rules and debate it afterwards.
>
> Castleford worked really hard and brought a lot to Super League and it's a shame for

them. All we could do was do our best to stay up, and winning four out of our last six games was the target. Four out of six has been achieved and Mission Impossible has been done.

John Kear, of course, was alluding amidst his deserved euphoria to the fact that Castleford had been relegated despite not coming bottom. The French side, Catalans Dragons, had fetched up at the foot of the table, closing with 16 points to the Tigers' 19, but had been given dispensation from the drop by those who run our game to help them build a solid base for the future. I'm just a player and political decisions such as that are for others to debate, but I'm sure I'd have felt sore if we'd lost to Castleford and had to go down despite finishing with more points than Catalans.

Maybe our leaders at Red Hall should ponder on the fact that livelihoods are at stake when a team is relegated, with many of the players having to look elsewhere for work, not to mention coaches and backroom staff. I suppose the Rugby Football League has to take a wider view, and they could point to the fact that teams have it in their own hands to get the number of wins needed to survive. Even so I suspect that people reading this book with no direct knowledge of rugby league will find the whole thing odd and will wonder if it would be allowed to happen in any other sport.

Those considerations weren't at the front of our thoughts on that late-summer Saturday in September. Initially drained, we partied long and hard into the night—and we'd every right to after recording what was surely one of the most important victories in Wakefield Trinity's proud history. The sensational success over Castleford, which I have to admit gave me a certain personal satisfaction after having been snubbed by the Tigers a few years earlier, capped a roller coaster ride stretching back over almost two months. John Kear, appointed coach on Monday 24 July, had only a couple of days earlier, witnessed a 42–20 defeat on our own patch at the hands of Bradford Bulls.

Jason Demetriou, Monty Betham and David Solomona had taken temporary charge of the side, with chief executive Steve Ferres fielding the post-match press conference amid rumours that former Castleford prop Dean Sampson could be poised to take over. Down 24–4 at half time, we at least gave the fans something to cheer with a more spirited display in the second period but Ferres admitted to it being the worst week in his 35 years in the game. With some foresight, he added: 'We've got two weeks to prepare now for Castleford and we will be looking forward to it. There are six games left; we hope that the results go our way this weekend and that the other teams don't get too far away.'

It was a theme picked up on by Kear less than 24 hours later. Given the coaching job at Belle Vue until the end of the season, with no guarantees about his employment prospects after that, he made no bones about the extent of the challenge facing both him and the players. He freely admitted that guiding us out of relegation trouble would equal his feats in winning the Challenge Cup with Sheffield Eagles in 1998 and with Hull FC eight years later. 'That was one of the main reasons I was delighted to take the job,' he said. 'It is a massive challenge but everyone at the club is really working hard towards the same goal. There are absolutely no worries about the desire of the players. It is all a matter of positive thinking and the players are determined to make things happen.'

What's remarkable, and perhaps too often overlooked, about John Kear's achievement is that he steered us out of the mire despite being unable to sign any new players. The transfer deadline had passed just three days before he put pen to paper on his deal at Trinity. The former Hull boss made light of that, 'We've got the personnel to do the job, that was one of the most appealing aspects in taking the post,' was the gratifying message that was certainly music to our ears as players. Kear also sorted out, quickly, one or two internal issues and, equally importantly, gave the players a new focus. He stressed that a run-in involving home and away games with Castleford, fixtures at St Helens and Bradford, and matches at Belle Vue against Leeds and Catalans, offered the possibility of 12 points. 'One win can transfer the pressure onto other sides and can build momentum. It's six games and we'll endeavour to win them all. If we're successful in that we'll be safe.'

He also concentrated on our defence, which had clearly been our big problem all season, stressing, 'When we get the ball in hand, I think we are as good as any side in Super League. But we've got to learn to be as good without the ball as we are with it. I think I have a bit of a reputation for reasonable defence structures in my sides and that will be important here.' John Kear was immediately true to his word, in every respect, in his first match as Wakefield's new boss. Having made light of the fact that he had—and still has—a lot of affection for the Castleford club with whom he had starred as a winger a couple of decades earlier, he proved that he wasn't being cavalier with the truth by masterminding an 18–0 win founded on strong defence. As he'd predicted this really did put pressure on our relegation rivals Castleford and Wigan. And what a victory it was, one which in the space of 80 minutes suddenly gave us all the belief that, under Kear, Super League survival was a real possibility, and maybe even more likely than not.

It was, almost literally, a magical win in that it was hard to make sense of. We had Kiwi loose forward Monty Betham sent off shortly before half time for getting over-excited in responding to Ryan McGoldrick's hand in his face, with substitute packman Ned Catic getting his marching orders two minutes from time for another red mist moment. My mate Danny Brough was a big absentee for Cas, maybe illustrating Kear's good fortune by being unavailable after copping a suspension for dissent a couple of weeks earlier. Kear sent out a clear warning signal to the sides above us when he said:

'I applaud the desire and commitment of my players. I think their character had been called into question before the game. The best way to answer that was to play the way we did. We've put the cat among the pigeons, and the victory has put us in reach of a clutch of other clubs. Those from seventh place down will be looking over their shoulders.'

We were only four points ahead when Betham departed, Semi Tadulala having scored in the first couple of minutes from a position established by a smart charge down by my half back partner Ben Jeffries, prop Michael Korkidas setting the platform for second row David Solomona to slip one of his special passes out of the tackle. I was unable to add the extras from wide out, and everyone in the ground, including the most partisan and optimistic of Wakefield Trinity Wildcats supporters, probably thought our future in Super League was non-existent when Mirfield referee Richard Silverwood sent Betham off.

But without Brough, Cas—who surprisingly failed to bring on Paul Handforth (an enterprising half back who stayed on the bench) and who could perhaps have done with Brad Davis on as a player rather than as a water carrier—lacked the invention to break our newly-resolute defence. Granted, we had an escape when Tigers winger Adam Fletcher had a 'try' in the corner ruled out for a forward pass by hooker Andrew Henderson, and we had a stroke of luck when full back Calum Halpenny nipped over from a pass by centre James Evans that to some (in the home crowd at any rate) looked equally illegal. We deserved our luck, and it certainly seemed to us that there was nothing wrong with a touchdown by our centre Ryan Atkins that was vetoed by the video referee. I was happy to give us a stronger platform with an angled kick which Evans ran onto to perfection, and we finished on a high when another former Tiger, Tommy Saxton, grabbed a late solo score. I added a goal to wrap up a vital win which had some of our loyal fans in floods of tears. Happily, they were tears of joy rather than the misery which would have engulfed Trinity in the event of defeat.

Suddenly, the mood had changed. John Kear's earlier reference to momentum was spot on and we now felt that the force was with us. Wigan, who had beaten Catalans 40–4, were still two points above us but something about the body language of the Castleford players and coaching staff—and their fans—smelled of relegation. We were beginning to enjoy this, one of the greatest challenges ever to have faced a Wakefield side and one, suddenly, to be relished. Our only worry was the possible suspensions to be imposed on Betham and Catic, but the news the following week that the pair had been banned for two and three matches respectively was at least tempered to some extent by the announcement that Wigan had been docked two points for breaching the salary cap the previous season. This happened following the signing of Great Britain prop Stuart Fielden, who had followed his old boss Brian Noble from Bradford Bulls to the JJB Stadium. Not that Wigan's punishment went down well at Belle Vue.

Steve Ferres made the point that if Wigan again stepped over the limit, any subsequent sanction, with double point penalties threatened by the Rugby Football League, would effectively apply in the wrong season and would be imposed too late to benefit their rivals. This would include possibly, us, although we were by now determined to make our own destiny and not rely too much on others. Having said that, we still needed our rivals to slip up and Wigan were clearly in no mood to grant us our wishes, winning 20–18 at Leeds the following Friday to register a seventh win in eight outings following Noble's arrival. The omens seemed, too, to be with the Pie Eaters, who would have been denied a point if Kevin Sinfield's late penalty attempt hadn't bounced out off a post.

The soothsayers, meanwhile, were having a field day at the Jungle, where Castleford were showing collective signs of panic and slumped to a 72–4 humbling at the hands of St Helens, for whom Aussie centre Jamie Lyon bagged 32 points with two tries and 12 goals. We, for our part, beat Catalans 34–14 at Belle Vue, despite the absence of Catic and Betham, and were now out of the relegation spot, above Wigan on points' difference but, perhaps more pertinently given the form of the teams in the relegation frame, only a point adrift of Castleford Tigers. Our forwards, with prop Michael Korkidas setting the agenda at the kick off with a great rampaging run, laid a great platform for Ben Jeffries and me at half back, and we both prospered against the Dragons.

I was able to grab a hat trick, and land seven

goals, to score 26 points, equalling my own record at Wakefield, but I could have done with a couple of those goals the following week, when it was Leeds' turn to come to Belle Vue. We lost 14–12, with both sides scoring two tries. I converted a touchdown by hooker David March, scored after I'd feinted to kick, and landed a penalty, but I was unable to convert Tommy Saxton's touchdown from the touchline. Wigan, meanwhile, won 14–10 against Huddersfield to go back above us; but those two results didn't seem to matter too much when Castleford were hammered 48–10 at Bradford. The final game of the season—Trinity against the Tigers—was already assuming massive significance and that view was given extra credence by the next set of results, after we'd all had a break for the Challenge Cup Final, in a sequence of which the master of suspense, Alfred Hitchcock, would have been proud.

John Kear—not surprisingly given the fact that he had won the Challenge Cup 12 months previously with Hull and was, at the moment, the flavour of the month with Wakefield Trinity Wildcats—was a guest summariser for the BBC for the clash between Huddersfield and St Helens at Twickenham. Our new boss was his usual articulate self in displaying quiet confidence for the three-game challenge (one as fraught as any Test series) ahead. The complexities surrounding the implications of relegation were highlighted, when we all swung back into action, by rumours coming out of the Jungle on the evening of Castleford's 27–12 victory over Harlequins that, should the Tigers stay up, our former Cronulla Sharks hooker Tevita Latu would be joining them. It's an issue that was never put to the test, although there was more concrete news regarding John Kear, who agreed a one-year extension to his deal with Wakefield, regardless of whether we survived or not.

While the Tigers won, we went down 34–12 at St Helens, and Wigan disposed of Bradford 38–16 to effectively seal their own top flight status. The results left us once more hanging onto Super League by a thread, three points behind Cas and with both teams having only two games remaining. Saints, on course for the 'treble' of the Challenge Cup, the Minor Premiership and the Super League title, were too strong for us in carving out a 34–12 success at Knowsley Road. John Kear was quick to keep our confidence high by giving us plenty of praise in his post-match press conference, stating that we played well enough to have beaten most other sides. We'd had a great start, too, Ben Jeffries and I opening up the home defence on several occasions in the early stages, and we took a deserved lead when I kicked a penalty, nosing further ahead when James Evans picked up my kick and linked with Jeffries to send Jason Demetriou over.

The Saints, though, hit back in the way only they can to lead 16–6 at the break, but we were back in it when Adam Watene powered over midway through the second half, my conversion reducing the deficit to only four points. But it all came to nothing, Ade Gardner collecting Sean

Long's kick to touch down, our hopes finally ending when Korkidas was sent off 16 minutes from full time for a head butt on Jamie Lyon. Kear said: 'I have to compliment my players on their character and commitment. They gave it in bucket loads tonight and they are fighting to the death in everything they do. We are down to the wire now and have to win the next two.'

The first of those was at Bradford Bulls the following week, and the scenario was quite simple. If Castleford could win at Salford, who were more or less assured of a top six spot, they would survive regardless of how we fared at Odsal. But if they lost at the Willows, and we could stage a surprise victory over the Bulls, then all would rest on our 'derby' clash at Belle Vue, although a draw would be enough for the Tigers to stay in the top flight at our expense. They say that truth can be stranger than fiction, and only a brave novelist (or John Kear) would conjure up the scorelines for the first weekend in September 2006. You've got to 'win ugly' sometimes and this was exactly such an occasion, a match described by *League Weekly*'s Danny Lockwood as a 'comedy of errors' and as 'the most inept professional rugby league it should be any paying customer's misfortune to see'. We didn't care about Lockwood's opinion of the quality on offer when, as the final hooter blew at Odsal with us 20–12 ahead, the news came over the tannoy that Castleford had gone down 26–16 at Salford. We'd got out of gaol, and it was celebration time with our loyal fans as most of the team leapt over the Odsal fencing to join in the joyous scenes on the terracing. Kear, at that moment, was telling the assembled hacks: 'I feel as if I've played every tackle. What that has done has put us into our own Grand Final. There is a feeling of satisfaction in our changing room, which comes from a group of players who are really working hard. Through that hard work, they've given themselves an opportunity. It was a heroic effort in the second half but we've got to keep our feet on the ground.'

That was difficult, that evening, as news emerged of the manner of Castleford's defeat. The Tigers, who had 2,000 fans at Salford, many taking advantage of free coach travel funded by the club, faced a tough task against a City Reds outfit that needed to win to make certain of a first-ever place in the play-offs. With the kick off delayed by 15 minutes to allow the 6,000-plus crowd in—something that didn't help our nerves as we waited at Odsal for the result—the tension was high. But Castleford looked good value for victory when they led 14–8 at half time. Salford rallied to lead 16–14 but Danny Brough levelled with a penalty and, with nine minutes left, it was anyone's game. Sadly for the Tigers—and happily for us—it turned out that the Reds did us a huge favour with late tries by Andy Coley and David Hodgson, Cas again ruing a referee when Karl Kirkpatrick vetoed a Luke Dyer effort in response. So we'd survived—but the truth is that it would have meant little or nothing if we'd failed to build on the achievement and gone down the following season.

Far from continuing to struggle the Wildcats have, under Kear, continued to progress and, quite apart from our Challenge Cup exploits of 2008, we are now a side with genuine Top Six aspirations. We have, since Kear's arrival, really taken off, and Wakefield Trinity are now habitually looking upwards rather than downwards. It's something I enjoy being part of, and I plan to be involved in it for quite a few years yet. One aspect that really draws me to the club is the excellent spirit among the players. We're a real family unit, which has been illustrated by the strong support from the lads for the Brennan Rooney Appeal, with their wives, girlfriends and children also getting behind us. The kids all seem to get on well with each other and you'll see them playing happily after matches. Most players will perform better if their family is happy, that's obvious I suppose, and it's been something that John Kear has focused on very much. He's keen on developing youth, as well, with a view to benefiting the club in the next three or four years. He isn't daft, he's been around at a few top clubs to know all this and we're reaping the rewards of his experience and expertise.

I haven't really thought about this too much, but when I reflect on it, the stability at Belle Vue has helped us in our efforts to get the necessary treatment for Brennan. With John Kear and the Wakefield board taking a long-term, structured approach to everything, both on and off the field, Erika and I haven't been distracted by the turmoil that seems to exist at so many clubs these days. So many coaches lose their jobs in Super League far too easily, John Kear himself lost his job at Hull despite winning the Challenge Cup. This stability has meant that our fundraising initiative to help meet the costs of Brennan's treatment has been much easier to organise. The fundraising was Erika's idea and I have to confess that I didn't go along with it at first. I had major doubts and she'd been talking about it for two or three years, maybe, before she turned me round. I suppose I was hesitant partly because I'm not into being the centre of attention, or asking people for money. For quite a while I viewed it as something I just didn't want to do, but in the end I realised that maybe I was being a bit selfish. In any case, it came to the point when we'd no alternative—we just had to go ahead with it and, looking back, it's the best thing I've done in my life. And looking at Brennan now, it's going to help him a huge amount.

In some ways it's like having a prolonged benefit. Some players take to the higher profile and regular events like a duck to water, while others don't. I'm, by nature, in the latter camp but it's worth it, for Brennan's sake, and everyone we come across has been unfailingly supportive. We've had some busy spells, there are periods when I've only been home for a couple of nights a week, with most evenings taken up by functions or rugby. I'm glad to say that my form didn't suffer during what was probably the most hectic period, in 2007, in fact it was exactly the opposite, with me gaining international recognition for the first time when I was selected to play for the Northern

Union side that took on the All Golds in the Centenary Test at Warrington.

You might argue that, rather than affecting me adversely, I performed better. In fact I think the way I started the season, you could say it was a bit of an inspiration to me. And it's not like benefit seasons; people have wanted to give me money. It's for a child, after all, and I don't think there's been an occasion, when we've asked people for donations, that they've said 'no'. We've never had to grovel, they've just given it. I've never had a testimonial, I'm still a bit young for that, thank goodness, but I think that would be different, because it would be for me. This is for a little child who's poorly, so it's not the same. I take the same view as everybody else, if I'm asked for money for poorly children, then I don't mind throwing a few quid in. I'd like to thank everybody who has helped, either by giving cash or by assisting in any other way. There's a real danger, of course, in naming names, because it's inevitable that someone always gets momentarily forgotten, so I'm going to avoid a litany of benefactors simply for that reason, other than mentioning a few who somehow typify the overwhelming support we've had.

High on the list are a couple of people I don't know and have never met. I couldn't believe it when a large cheque arrived through the post when the fund was first launched, accompanied by a short note. The cash had been sent by Thomas and Jamie, of Bradford, and from their writing it looked as though they were children themselves.

Martin Sowerby, meanwhile, has been fantastic in overseeing fundraising events and it's largely through his sterling and tireless efforts that we'd raised almost £100,000 by Christmas 2007. Jimmy Gittins at leading amateur club Sharlston, who broke his back in a game a few years ago, went out of his way to organise a sponsored run for us, and that was tremendous, while boxer Ricky Hatton donated a pair of his gloves for auction. Manchester United offered Brennan the chance to be a mascot at one of their games at Old Trafford and although the initiative didn't come off for various reasons the gesture was genuinely made and much appreciated. We're secretly hoping that there may be some kind of mix-up and that Wayne Rooney's royalty payments from his book somehow find their way through to our account, and vice versa! Former St Helens and Hull player Steve Prescott, who is suffering from cancer, has been an inspiration and we were moved by his sponsored walk. I mustn't forget how Erika lost a stone in an hour and a half doing an 11-mile run!

So there is so much we have to be grateful for and although life in general hasn't always been straightforward—is it for anyone?—I'm very happy with my lot and I can't have any real complaints. Being a professional rugby player is a great life, it's a blessing to have a career doing what you love. To me, getting up in the morning and going training isn't work. I'm getting out of bed with the prospect of learning new things to better myself on the rugby field. That's not graft, it's play-time really, rather than work, and I can't believe my luck in getting paid for something I love.

We can have a laugh in training, too. Some fans say that there aren't so many characters in the game these days, but they only see players on a Sunday afternoon. When you're in a match you can't laugh, joke and lark around, although there are moments, of course. But through training every day you get to know people and their characters, and believe you and me there are some characters out there.

I just enjoy my life and I wouldn't change anything. I know Brennan's in a difficult situation but he also enjoys his life. As I write this section, it's almost Christmas 2007, and Brennan and Fletcher are both very aware that Santa's coming next week. I think it will be a special Christmas for us this year, with Bren going to Germany soon, following the excellent news, which came through on his birthday, about his hips. That was a very big day for us and although Erika is as tough as old boots, if you mention anything about Brennan she gets very emotional. To get the news she did about his hips, on that day especially, well, she must have thought Christmas had come early. I'm just hoping this time next year, on his birthday, we'll get some more good news.

9

CHALLENGING
TIMES

When Erika flew out to Germany, together with
Brennan, Fletcher and her mum, Lynn, I really
thought I'd be able to hold it all together. I'm
generally a composed sort of bloke. I've had my
share of knocks in life, like lots of other people,
and I suppose that's helped me keep my chin up
when times get tough. I'd hoped when seeing my
family fly off without me I'd remain calm and
reasonably collected. It wasn't to be. As the
moment arrived it just seemed to get to me. When
I saw my kids and better half going off for three
months I found it hard, there's no getting away
from it. I don't think Brennan and Fletcher will
have realised how broken up I was—I hope they
didn't—but Erika can read me like a book and she
certainly knew.

The main thing, though, was to keep my distress
hidden from our lads and I think I did that. But I
was a bit of an emotional wreck all the way home.
It's hard to admit that a grown man can cry, but
when your family is involved it's very difficult. It's
normally me leaving the country for a few days,

going to training camps and what have you, but when it was them leaving for a different country, especially in the circumstances that were involved, it was pretty testing. Erika's dad, Brian, and her niece Taylor were also there to see them off, and we were all very upset.

But having said all that, and I told myself this at the time, it was a dream come true in many ways. The chance for Brennan to get the treatment that could change his life for the better was not one we could miss out on or remotely pass up. So there was no real choice in the issue, no matter how harrowing the moment of parting might be. The amazing thing was that it all happened more or less purely by chance. Erika had been watching morning TV one day, only half watching it really if truth be told, as she was getting Brennan and Fletcher ready. I think it was Fern and Phil's programme, and the subject of cerebral palsy came up, which naturally drew her attention. A lad who looked a bit like Brennan, only he was a bit older, was on the sofa with them. They were talking about this place they'd been to in Poland, and they were waxing lyrical about how brilliant it was. Erika said straight away that we'd have to look into it, and the whole thing developed from there.

Another family, Mark, Toni and Georgia Head from London, had seen the show, and they went on to attend the centre in Poland. They came up to see us, having read an article about Brennan in the *News of the World*, and they were fantastic, really helpful. It's striking though, after we'd spent so much time talking to so many experts and trawling around various centres, how this—our main source of hope so far—happened so much by chance. It was fortunate, too, that the centre in question had moved from Poland to Germany, to the small town of Ratingen, near Dusseldorf, which is that bit closer to us. We couldn't help getting the feeling that perhaps everything was falling into place.

My feelings as I drove back home from the airport were that, as with the fundraising, which was continuing to go well, we were up and down all the time on a real roller coaster ride, to borrow a well-worn cliché. Although it was hard for Erika and the boys to be away for three months, it would be worth it in the end. There wasn't really any alternative, it was as simple as that in the final analysis. Erika had had a schedule mapped out in which they'd go to the centre from their apartment, which was only 10 minutes' walk away, for a three and a half hour session each morning, six days a week, for 12 weeks. I planned to fly out twice a month or so, after matches, to spend a day or two with them. Erika would be there with her mum for seven weeks, then my mum would have a week out there; Erika's sisters, Jessica and Rebecca, and niece Taylor, were also popping over.

It was harder being on my own than I'd expected. I worried all the while about them all being over in Germany without me—and the situation wasn't helped by a drop in my rugby form. The first two months that they were away coincided with the toughest couple of months of my career, and I missed them badly. Erika's a real rock for me off the field; when things aren't going so well on the pitch she always lifts me up and gives me that bit of confidence, and it was hard without them being at home. When I did manage to get over to see them, it was generally just for a day, because I had to be back for training. It was great to see them, but that was tempered by the fact that it was even harder coming back home within 24 hours. I tended to fly over on the Sunday, returning to England on Monday night, and by the time I arrived at the apartment in Germany the kids were in bed anyway, so I only got to see them for a day. Initially, we weren't sure how long we'd be staying, we wouldn't have a clear idea on that until the physios had had their say on Brennan's progress. Even now, we're not sure, and that's how it will continue until his course of treatment eventually ends.

During the first week or two, after Erika and the kids had gone, it was nice to get a bit of peace and quiet, even if it could get a little lonely. I was able to put my feet up when I wanted, watch whatever I fancied on the telly, and have whatever I fancied to eat. That's not bad for a few days but it didn't make up for being without my family and after a month or two it got hard. A lot of people were saying that the time had flown but for me it seemed as though they'd been away forever. It got to the point, in fact, that I wished they were back home, and that there was a place in England we could visit instead of having to travel all the way to Germany. But that might not have been so very different unless there had been somewhere nearby in Yorkshire and I reconciled myself to how it had to be—I had to look at the positives as well as at Brennan's future. That's what was getting Erika through it, really, over there. The only option has to be the right option. We didn't want to find ourselves looking back in years to come having to say that we didn't follow it through simply because we were missing each other. There were no ifs and buts, it's something we had to do.

Erika, to be fair, did brilliantly well out there in Germany. She kept on smiling and joking, she's such a strong person and she was doing what's best for Brennan. It was hard work for him, though. He never has 'sleeps' in the afternoon at home, but he did in Germany, which showed how much the morning sessions were taking out of him. The kid was trying his best all the time, but it was always going to be hard for him because he wasn't used to moving some of the muscles that they were trying to make him use. Those muscles were very weak and that made it hard for him. But he's a strong lad who was doing his best and Erika and I were, and still are, proud of him, and of what he was doing.

His education was unfortunately a little bit on hold, but getting him mobile was the priority and our view was that he'd always be able to catch up, over time, on his work when he got back. He's smarter than he lets on. The worst thing, perhaps, about Germany was that there wasn't very much for them all to do. They did the same walk every day. I went on it with them when I flew over, and Erika was of course helping Brennan out with his schoolwork, but they had no transport. Erika wouldn't drive a hire car, she's got a thing about driving over here, never mind in Germany and although there are trams and busses, it can be difficult getting Brennan on and off them.

Brennan found it the hardest of all of us, of course. His exercises were hard work, and it wasn't easy for him being away from home, where he tends to feel safe. When he's somewhere he doesn't know with different people messing around with him all the time, he can struggle a little. The TheraSuitReha Centre is quite small, very clean, has three rooms for treatment and a bigger room acting as a reception. There are only two physios based at the centre, Brennan's physio, Tomasz, who works alongside the other physio, Katarzyna. During his first trip to Germany, they were good to him, we knew that and we were aware that they knew their jobs. We hadn't, and never have had, any complaints whatsoever about how they have looked after him. Their approach has been unfailingly professional and exemplary. But Brennan was at an age when he didn't really understand what they were doing to him, or why. He would just look at Erika as if he was asking for help, as if he wanted her to stop them from doing whatever they were doing.

Erika's tough, but even she found that hard. We told him it was for his own good, even though it was a struggle, but we weren't at all sure whether he appreciated what we were saying. He's been brought up with exercises really, we started doing them as soon as we found out about his condition, when he was just a year old, so it's something he's very much used to. It was a lot harder for him over in Germany, a real step up from what he was used to, and we had to be brave for him. Erika had to leave the room, and let them get on with doing the exercises, because I think her being there made him worse. That was tough for her. We both, but me especially, kept asking ourselves whether we were doing the right thing for Brennan. I'm like Erika, I hate seeing him in pain and it was a bit of a roller coaster ride, one minute he was up, the next he was down. Sometimes he actually laughed through his exercises, believe it or not, but more typically he'd do his first couple of hours and then start screaming.

Against all that, not being selected for Wakefield Trinity Wildcats in the early stages of the 2008 season was all I needed. John Kear declared me unfit, with a shoulder injury, but I felt I was okay. He was the boss at the end of the day, so what he said went, but it wasn't easy at all being on the sidelines. I get paid to play rugby, and I enjoy the game. It's something I love doing and it's tough sitting in the stands, helplessly watching. As a player, I felt fit, so it became a selection issue for me, rather than an injury issue. Fair play to John, the players who had been turning out for the Wildcats had been playing well. Not being picked is a good test of character. I always want my side to win, and I hate them to lose even if I've not played. All players, even top players, have been dropped in their career. It's how they react, and how they bounce back, that matters. I must admit that, with the family being away, it was hard not having them there to pick me up. Erika doesn't ever let me mope around, she'll put me in my place. She tried to put me right on the phone and when I went over to Germany she sorted me out again with a good kick up the arse.

John Kear has been extremely supportive. He's a very shrewd coach, he knows what he's doing and his man-management is first class. After what he's done for me, Brennan and my family, you'll never hear me say a bad word about him. He may have left me out partly because of family issues. There could have been something in that behind his selections, but whilst the team were successful it was difficult to argue with him. It wouldn't have been fair on the lads who had played instead to get dropped, because they'd been performing well. We're all professionals, and we all want to play, it's just a matter of biding time, training hard and when the chance comes again, making the most of the opportunity and proving you're worth a place in the side.

One of my problems was that we had a good victory over Bradford Bulls on the opening day of the season, without my involvement. We always seem to play well against the Bulls. Their previous fixture had been in the play-offs in 2007 when coach Steve McNamara paid a high price for withdrawing several key players early in the second half against Wigan, believing that they had already won the match. They hadn't and Wigan blasted back from almost 30 points down to snatch a sensational victory. Against that background Bradford would have been doubly determined to get off the mark at the first time of asking in the 2008 campaign. On our own patch especially we can be a real team. Maybe the Bulls were off the boil, having had only one pre-season friendly. We'd had five, and we hit the ground running, while the Odsal outfit appeared to be undercooked. We outplayed them all over the park—the result was a good win and a fine start to the season against a side which, bolstered by some astute signings, I expected to be challenging for the Super League title. For us to play well enough to beat them was a real boost and one which hopefully would set the tone for a real and sustained challenge for the top six.

I pondered on this some nights when I was sitting at home on my own twiddling my thumbs. I do watch a lot of sport on telly, and Erika tends to go mad with me for watching sport all the time, but with nobody around at least I was able to take in as much as I liked. I must have been on the sports channels all the time, and I had some of the lads round, watching football. I've always trained longer than the other players. We train in the morning, starting around 8.30am with weights, with a field session about 12.30. There are video sessions to fit in between, and it was nice to be around the lads while the family was away.

I'm usually home for 2.30pm to 3.00pm after staying behind for goal-kicking practice, and I extended that to take up a bit of extra time. I cleaned every room in the house repeatedly, to the extent that I started to worry that Erika would wonder what had been going on when she got back to find an ultra-tidy house. We'd decided to have an extension done and dealing with the builders took up some time, as did making them cups of tea. I also watched any sport that was on the telly. Darts, rugby union, soccer, cricket, you name it, anything. Erika would have gone spare! Although I obviously spend a lot of time thinking about rugby, watching other sports does take my mind off it. That was probably the hardest part about it, just coming home and that's all I was thinking about, rugby. In particular, I was dwelling on not playing, which makes you think about the game even more. So, in those circumstances, it can be good to get home and watch a different sport for a change.

Although my family were hundreds of miles away, I was able to talk to them every day through the wonders of web cam. Brennan laughed sometimes when he heard my voice, while on other occasions he would get a bit upset. The truth was that he wanted to come home in the early stages. He had to do his exercises, something he was used to up to a point, but over there they pushed him a lot harder than he'd been used to— more than we thought they would. Hopefully, in a few years' time, he will understand why we've done it and thank us for it. I wanted him back myself, together with Erika and Fletcher. The strangest thing was leaving the house in the morning and coming back in the afternoon to find it exactly the same. Normally there would be toys all over the room, and pots everywhere where they'd been eating. But the worst thing was simple boredom, more than anything, although my working hours, if I can call them that, gave me the chance to help out other members of the family. I'd pick up Taylor, Brennan's cousin, from school sometimes and look after her for a few hours. She would talk to her auntie Erika on the web cam and have a chat with Brennan and Fletcher. This would always put a smile on Brennan's face.

Then I'd go shopping, but that was strange as well, although I don't mind doing food shopping. I often go to a local farm or nip to the supermarket, but it was odd not getting stuff in for the kids. I couldn't get out of the habit of getting up at 4.00am, looking round and expecting Fletcher to be up. I was struggling to sleep at one stage, which I hadn't expected. I'd imagined that because they weren't at home I'd have the chance for loads of sleep. So I was thrown well out of kilter, what with one thing and another, but I knew it was all going to be worth it. We were presented with evidence of that before our very eyes. A little girl at the centre was walking, although she was a lot older than Brennan, and that raised our hopes. She knew why she was there, which is what Brennan was still coming to terms with. There were many things he was struggling to understand; for one thing, his mum usually does his exercises with him, so he would have been wondering why she wasn't doing them anymore and who this strange man was that was doing them with him in her place.

That was one of the points. Erika, when putting Brennan through his exercises, had always stopped when he'd started to cry. In Germany they simply carried on through it, because that was an essential part of the treatment. She found that tough and, as already mentioned, eventually they had to ask her to leave the room, because her presence was making it harder for Brennan. She told me that it was heartrending in the first few weeks, he would scream for the full four hours and look at her as if to say, 'Tell them to stop, mummy'. Her instinct, naturally, was to pick him up and cuddle him, love him and give him a rest, but she had to stand there and watch as the therapists tried to motivate him into doing the exercises, with Brennan making no effort at all to co-operate. But as Brennan got to know the physiotherapist, Tomasz, better he began to co-operate more and gradually took to him.

Meanwhile Erika had to go and sit in reception on her own; heartbroken and isolated from everybody because they were all German-speaking. I think that got to her a bit, although it couldn't be helped. She struggled as she had no idea what people were talking about, whether in the centre, in the supermarket or just out in the street. We were pleased when Tomasz did Brennan's two-month assessment. The only real issue was that Brennan, being so young, didn't understand why he was going through the ordeal, so it was going to take a little longer than they'd anticipated, but they were certainly happy with his progress. He couldn't help his age although the reverse side of the coin was that being young gave him something of a head start.

While I was bored at home, they were all equally bored in Germany, especially as it rained almost constantly for the first eight weeks. They were stuck inside their apartment for most of the time with little to do. Fletcher, having no one to play with, had to be entertained and it wasn't easy for any of them until the weather got a bit better and they found a country park with horses and sheep and a little swimming pool. They also went on the tram to Dusseldorf a couple of times. This was difficult because once Brennan finished his treatment, had his sleep and completed his schoolwork, it was heading for teatime, leaving very little time for anything else. Being with the children every hour of the day, and with Brennan not sleeping very well, meant Erika was at the end of her tether. Both Erika and her mum, who had left her husband at home for three months, were finding it hard. Everybody was out of sync, and it didn't help that no one at all in the village seemed to speak English, and that none of us speak German. Very often, people do speak English when you're abroad, but it was not the case there, so it was hard for Erika to go into restaurants and order food. She's not allowed to have anything with flour in it either—she has a gluten-free diet and that's hard to explain if you don't speak the language. One treat they had every weekend was to go a Chinese restaurant and the real highlight of each day was simply waiting for the post, which says a lot. There were memorable incidents, however. On their very first day there, they went to the supermarket. Erika was in the queue waiting to pay. Her mum (Lynn) and Fletcher went to stand out of the way when an elderly woman suddenly started shouting, and waving her finger at Lynn. They had no idea what she was saying and Lynn just stood there, stunned. All Erika could do was laugh—they think, although they can't be sure, that the pensioner was accusing them of pushing in. That was a strange event and people in Germany can be very rude—or it comes across like that, maybe because they have different ways to us. Only one woman took the time to stop and try to chat, with a simple, 'Good morning,' each day. She tried to talk to Brennan, but everyone else just tried to avoid them or look away. The impression we got was that they were cold people. That may be unfair; perhaps we've been spoilt by living in Featherstone, a close-knit community in which everyone knows everyone else and people aren't backwards at coming forwards. It may have just been the area; there was no problem with people in Dusseldorf, Erika thinks it was just that one little town.

The big incident was when they managed to get themselves locked out of the apartment. It was when my mum, Karen, was over and there was a mix-up over who had the keys. The keys were actually inside the door and when it shut, with everyone on the outside, they had a problem. Erika put a key in from the outside, to knock the original key out, but the new one snapped. This was, by any stretch of the imagination, a stressful situation, given that it was 4.50pm and the shops were closing. They went to a key shop first but couldn't make themselves understood, so they hurried off to the shop they'd rented the apartment from. Fortunately the man there was nice and helped them out, organising a locksmith who got them back in; but it did cost a couple of hundred Euros.

Then it happened again, only this time Erika was with her mum, Lynn. On this occasion, though, the shops were shut, and the key hadn't been left in the other side of the lock. They'd gone back after having been out for a walk to get Brennan changed before going out for tea. Erika had chucked the keys onto a chair, when the door slammed shut. She was walking up the street and, by a stroke of luck, the bloke who worked in the shop was walking down the other way—otherwise it's hard to think what exactly they would have done. The shop was closed for the night, but he helped them out again, and this time they didn't have to pay. They were lucky. Erika says they were like headless chickens.

All this was, we're sure, going over the head of Fletcher, who was too young to know why he was in a different place. He didn't even know that he'd been going over to Germany, but Brennan did. Fletcher tends to be all over Brennan all the time, he loves him to bits. We weren't worried about Fletcher because he adapts to anything. He was at the age that as long as he was looked after and fed, he didn't care much about anything. Brennan was more aware. There was the time, a few months before he went to Germany for his treatment, when I went to a training camp for four days. Brennan was in the car with Erika and a song came on by Akon and he said, 'Daddy' and suddenly realised that I'd gone. He started crying and Erika struggled to settle him down. She rang me and, luckily, I answered—which doesn't always happen as I have trouble with mobiles—and that was enough, he was alright then.

He wasn't alright in the early stages in Germany. During the first few weeks he wasn't himself. It became clear that it wasn't merely a change of environment; he wasn't well, and after a visit to the doctor we found out why. He had an ear infection. Fletcher, meanwhile, was banned from the centre. He was too boisterous, and the children couldn't concentrate from laughing at him jumping about the place. They found a little park to take him to, and he was delegated to helping in the flat with dinner and (ha ha) cleaning! He's a loving brother, and as soon as Brennan got back from the centre he'd be all over him, shouting, 'Hello brother, hello brother!'

He really does cause havoc. The first time I saw him I was a bit worried to be honest, because he was quiet, not himself at all at that stage, but he picked up a lot once he got settled and quickly became his same old self. He always puts a smile on your face and while he didn't know what was going on, that was probably a good thing really. We were hoping that it wouldn't affect him and that he'd still want to join in with things at nursery when he came home; we needn't have worried, he always has to get involved.

We did consider keeping Fletcher in England with me but we soon realised it wasn't realistic. It wouldn't have worked for many reasons. Brennan needed him for starters, he's always talking about Fletcher and he'd have missed his brother more than anybody. They do need to be together really at such times. I don't think Erika could have left him with me, which was another thing; it would have been hard on her as well. She needed her boys with her as it was hard enough out there without having to worry about what might have been going on in England with Fletcher. Not that Fletcher always helped. He'd tap Brennan on the head, saying, 'Come on brother,' and he'd get upset when Bren was crying. There were occasions, too, when he smacked people; sometimes he could get a little bit out of hand. It was nothing too serious but this still needed addressing and he had to sit on the naughty step a few times.

The impressive progress made by Brennan in the first couple of months, made clear by Tomasz's positive report, was a massive boost after a terrible first six weeks in which Erika often felt like packing her bags and coming home. In those first few weeks she continually questioned herself about whether we'd done the right thing, often thinking that perhaps we hadn't. Everything seemed to be difficult—for example the language problems with Tomasz not speaking much English and none of us speaking Polish or German. This meant we had to use an interpreter, Ola, who went with Erika, Brennan and Fletcher to Dusseldorf just to be friendly and helpful. This summed up how supportive they were at the centre. It's quite difficult when dealing with medical matters. If Tomasz needed to tell Erika anything, he'd say it to Ola, who would pass it on, and Erika would reply through Ola, who didn't understand all the medical terms. Because of that, it wasn't always easy for Ola to understand what Tomasz was getting at exactly, and then work out how to explain it to Erika. That wasn't anybody's fault, but it was quite difficult. Brennan really got to like her; she was classed as an entertainer as well as an interpreter, and her role was partly to keep the kids happy. She certainly did that.

We were all glad that the Heads were in Germany for a while, too. Toni and Mark's daughter Georgia had done very well and had begun to walk, so they'd been going there for much shorter periods. Erika really appreciated them when they were there; they were more helpful than you could imagine, pointing out the local supermarket and the places to eat with English menus, and sharing nights out. It was better for me when Wakefield played on Friday evenings. Fixtures scheduled for early in the weekend gave me the chance to spend three days in Germany, which I snapped up. Brennan seemed to respond really well when I went over after we'd played (and unfortunately lost to) Leeds. He shouted out for me when I went to the centre, and he barely cried all day. Erika thinks he was showing off a bit, and when it was time to do the walking he did it brilliantly and repeatedly asked to do it again. There was real praise from Tomasz, who said he had done 'super' and that clearly meant a lot to Bren.

Brennan, Erika and Fletcher enjoyed visits from other members of the family. A big highlight was a visit from Erika's sister, Jessica, her friend Kerry and Taylor. Taylor is very close to the boys, a real little stalwart and their arrival was a massive boost. My visits were a boost when I arrived with a case full of much-missed 'goodies' which are hard to obtain in Germany. I felt as though I was someone from the Red Cross, and I'm glad I wasn't stopped at the airport. I know there is nothing illegal about what I was taking over, but I'd have felt a bit silly explaining away dozens of packets of cheese strings. Customs officers would have wondered exactly what was going on, but I suppose they see stranger things.

I booked seven flights in a block from Leeds-Bradford, because it was cheaper that way, but they don't fly on Saturdays so when I played on Fridays, I waited until Sunday night to go over which meant losing two days. I tended to use my return flight from Leeds-Bradford on the Monday, and buy another ticket out of Manchester early on the Saturday morning, to arrive in Germany at around 8 or 9. It cost a bit more, but it meant being there for three days rather than only one. It was worth it and much better than simply sitting around at home. This gave us more time to talk properly about things like the extension, which otherwise we were dealing with over the web cam. I held materials up for Erika to decide about things such as the flooring from a small screen. They had to watch my matches on the small screen as well, which wasn't ideal but better than nothing, even if it was more like having the radio on than the telly. Erika hadn't quite realised before she set off how much she'd miss some things that she took for granted, such as rugby and, of course, her Strongbow. She really looked forward to watching matches at the weekend, although she had to settle for gin and tonic to replace her favourite cider.

Meanwhile, I was lamenting my shoulder injury, which to a degree was self-inflicted. I did it against Catalans Dragons, towards the end of the 2007 season, chasing my hat trick try—and I wasn't going to give up on the chance of that. I got it okay, but the trouble was that Ben Jeffries was going for the ball as well. He landed on my shoulder, and it didn't do it any good at all. I needed an operation, but I had to put that on hold because of my call up for England. I continued playing with pain-killing injections, and it felt okay when the 2008 season got under way and I played against St Helens in a friendly. I was a bit cagey, obviously, holding back a bit I think, and perhaps that showed in my performance. Whatever the reason was, I wasn't at my best, but that's what friendlies are for really, to help blow off the cobwebs and get any rustiness out of the system. Unfortunately, the season started the following week, and John Kear didn't think my shoulder was up to it. He left me out for the Bradford game, the lads played pretty well, and that was it—you don't change a winning side.

If you're not selected there's always the Under 21s team, which can include six over-age players. Match fitness is important of course, and it's an avenue used to keep players in shape, but having said that I do think the Under 21s is more for young kids to come through, and have a crack, than for older players like me. After three or four weeks outside the first team, yes, I'd then want to play in the Under 21s, I wouldn't want to go off the boil altogether. It's a good thing it's there for players coming back from injury or trying to recover form but happily it never came to that. It's not easy being out of the first team and the way a senior player—or any player for that matter—reacts is very important to the squad as a whole. We are split up at Wakefield if we're not in the side; John Kear likes to focus on moves with the 17 first team players, which is understandable. The problem then, though, can be that the others feel that they are not part of it. I try to stay positive, mainly for the rest of the lads. I don't want them to see me down in the dumps, I try to give them a boost and keep their spirits up, give them a bit of confidence, and help them as much as I can.

It's not possible to do anything else. There are players who sulk but at the end of the day sulking doesn't get you back in the side. It's not helping the team, and it's not the other players' fault that you're not in the team. It's the coach's decision. I always like to help the players out, I'm getting to an older age group now, it's important I set an example and if I can help in any shape or form I will. Even if I'm not playing I'll still try to do my bit for the team, and I still want us to win—I'm not one of those who wants to see their team get hammered, thereby making a point, if they get left out.

Everybody gets dropped at some stage in their career. It's not possible to play at the highest level week-in, week-out; there is bound to be a time when a player has a dip in form. With the squads clubs have these days, it only takes a couple of weeks of not playing quite at your best and someone will chomp at the bit to replace you. All a player can do in that situation is help as much as he can, and train hard. Moping around feeling sorry for yourself won't get you back in the side, far from it. I stayed out after training and put bombs up for the wingers and the full backs, helping them out that way. I did moves and plays with them to give the young kids a confidence boost through talking to them positively. Players are just as much part of the side even if they're not picked as if they are in the line up. I've known players who, after being dropped, have gone around slagging off other players and their team-mates. You never see or hear from them again, their career just disappears, and rightly so. Attitude is a big part of sport, or of life, and you've got to have the right approach in rugby league. You're always going to have downs in life, and it's

BORDERS BIRSTALL

FUTURE RUGBY LEAGUE SIGNINGS

PETER FOX Saturday May 2nd 1pm onwards. Peter will be signing copies of his autobiography "The Players Coach". Peter Fox was in rugby league for 50 years with Sharlston Rovers, Batley, Hull KR and Wakefield Trinity.

MAURICE BAMFORD Saturday 16th May 1pm onwards. Rugby legend now rugby writer Maurice will be signing his brand new book "One Hundred Winters" and signing his other books.

KRIS RADLINSKI Saturday 20th June 1pm onwards. One of the all time great rugby league full back players Kris Radlinski will be signing his autobiography "Simply Rad".

All signings subject to change at short notice please check with the store on 01924 474914.

how you deal with them that matters.

In any case, the reality is that it invariably comes down to the player himself. Even when I got back in the team, I wasn't happy with the way I was playing. I hadn't set Super League alight in the way I had at the start of the previous season. In the position I play, I like to be in the headlines, scoring tries, landing important drop goals, having a real and positive impact in various ways, and it wasn't happening. For whatever reason things just weren't going right for me. I'd been determined not to let the fact that my family were away in Germany and worries over Brennan affect my form. At the time I couldn't see why it should but, with hindsight, perhaps it was inevitable. I didn't think it was affecting me but, looking back, it obviously took its toll on me a little. I don't want to use it as an excuse, but I suppose it was a reason, I'm only human after all.

I desperately missed having my family around and I found it difficult to get out of thinking negatively about my form. In these circumstances I started questioning my ability. A hundred things started going through my head, most of which would have been better not entering it in the first place. When Erika's around she doesn't give me chance to think like that, there's always stuff to do and there isn't a minute to start brooding. People say you shouldn't dwell on things but when it's your job and there's nothing else in your life to take it away, it's pretty difficult. I tried to think about Brennan, and then became upset about him not being home. Those were the worst few months of my rugby career, without a doubt. But I still felt positive about the future, for Brennan and for my rugby. I could see a decent partnership developing at half back with Danny Brough, and we've become good mates. I knock about with him in training, he's a character and a cocky little half back, and he's got a buzz on and off the field. I think he brings the best out in me, and keeps me on my toes. I pick up a few tries off his passing and his kicking; that's my game really, playing off the back of breaks by other players.

Broughie, Brad Drew and I are three players with good kicking games, which isn't bad at all. That makes it hard for the opposition to pick up on who will be kicking. The previous year it was just Ben Jefferies and me, so other teams knew where we were coming from. That maybe sums up why things are looking good at Wakefield Trinity Wildcats. To play well every week there needs to be competition for places. Everyone has to be at their best. That's what we've got; we know that if we don't perform we can be sitting on the sidelines the week after. That can only be good for the team and the club. And it's got to be good for the players; being dropped gave me the kick up the backside that I needed.

There are inevitably downs in sport and in life, and I've probably had a fair few. It's the same with Erika. It's the way you bounce back that matters. Erika's gone through the same thing with Brennan. I don't think we could have had a bigger low than we've had with him, and the way she's responded has been amazing, a real inspiration.

There's no point feeling sorry for ourselves, that's not going to help our eldest son. After knock backs such as my dad's death and Brennan's diagnosis, not being picked for a rugby team, even though it's my job, seems like a little problem. It's up to me to solve that problem. My dad's death and Brennan's condition were both out of my hands— I could do nothing about either of them. Being dropped from the team was down to me and if anyone was to be blamed it was me. I'm not one to let my head drop and feel sorry for myself. I just focus on training hard and hopefully get a chance.

I'm happy at Wakefield and I couldn't really see myself anywhere else, although players never know in this game. A club might think they don't need a player anymore, so the player has to find another club or another club might come in. But the big decision isn't just about me, it's about my family and how it would affect them. For example if London came in, they could offer the world but I think my answer would have to be, 'No'. A single lad probably wouldn't think twice but family has to come first. I like to be a stone's throw away from the family, just in case anything happens and I need to get home.

Tommy Smales always gives me words of wisdom and puts things in perspective. When I talk to him he makes me think, 'What am I moaning about, there's nothing to worry about?' I like to see him a couple of times a week: he sorts out my niggling injuries and he makes me realise that although I've been dropped, at the end of the day it's just a game of rugby. There's more to life, such as a child's education. Going to Germany to improve Brennan's condition is great, but it inevitably impacts on his education and his school is getting concerned, which is as it should be. They've been saying that we're not meeting his statement, and suggesting that we put him in a school in Germany each day after his treatment.

At the moment they're letting Erika teach him, but there are logistical problems in Germany which will be hard to overcome. Ratingen is only a small town, little more than a village really, so if he goes to a school which has the facilities to educate him, by the time Erika gets him there after a morning's treatment the day will have gone. There's also the fact that after his morning session he's simply too tired, and needs a sleep. An option would be for him to go to school first, but the question then arises as to whether he'd be too tired after a morning's work to undergo a session. We're not sure he could tolerate it. The school asked if we could take him to Germany in the holidays so he doesn't miss as much as he has been doing. The centre shuts in August, so 2009 could be the first opportunity. On top of that, the people at the centre need their own family time. They work six days a week and they have a little girl, she's three years old, and they're Polish, so they've moved away from their own family and set up in Germany. They know how we feel because they're in the same situation. They have been very understanding and caring; we feel very comfortable there, and that makes a big difference.

It's been very tough. When I was over in Germany I found watching Brennan doing his exercises hard because he was crying and screaming. I can't really imagine what Erika and her mum Lynn had to go through, watching him day after day. But we knew why he was there, and what we had to do to make it work. They did stretching exercises, but more intense than normal, from 9.00am through to 12.30pm, without any break. That would be hard enough for me, really, and I'm a Super League player, so it must have been very hard for Brennan. And there was little respite when he came home for a month— Erika had to keep up the exercises as much as she could, or all his progress could have gone to waste.

10

BETTER FORTUNES

It was a tough time when Brennan first went to Germany, there's no question about that, but I'd no doubt in my own mind, and I knew that Erika felt the same way, that taking him there would prove to be the best thing we've ever done. We had to remind ourselves, especially when things became hard, that it was all for his long-term benefit, and that it would stay that way for quite some time. The physios planned periodic assessments, from which they'd determine how long he could return to England for before going back to Germany, and how long he would have to be there before coming back home. We understood from the outset that we'd be returning for the next five to 10 years. Eventually the visits would be for shorter periods.

That's what happened for the Heads, who were fantastic with Erika and me when we both went to look around the centre in November 2007. They invited her over and she had a good look around their apartment and the centre. That chance to asses everything was invaluable. Tomasz and Katarzyna (his wife) hadn't any equipment at that stage—they have now—but they showed her videos of it, and told her what we'd be doing while we were there. She got a good feel of what it would be like, and when she came home we felt a lot better about the whole thing. We met the two therapists who would be doing the treatment, who were nice. Mark Head's wife, Toni, was going to be there the following February as well, so there was a full month when they'd be there to show us where everything was, such as the best places to eat. They'd been going for two years, and they'd a much better idea of the town.

Erika and her mum didn't feel as isolated as they would have done otherwise. They felt daunted when they went over for the first time, but not as daunted as they might have done, and it was better for me as well. I felt much more comfortable, having some idea of what they were facing, plus the fact that we'd bought a laptop with a web cam facility meant we could keep in contact better than otherwise. I would be having a bowl of rice on my own on Saturday nights, as part of my pre-match preparations, while they would be going for a Chinese—not much sympathy there for me from Erika! The plan was that at least I'd get some sleep. I'd drift off comfortable in the knowledge that there were children at the centre who had been going for years and that as time passed the periods they went for had shortened. Some of the children had progressed to the walking stage, but they were still going because their parents wanted to see more improvement. That's the kind of positive feedback we got and it was inspiring.

Some of the children were walking with sticks, for short distances admittedly, but the fact was that they were walking and that they kept returning and improving. It's one of those situations where if they didn't keep going, they could fall back a bit, which is something I can relate to as a professional sportsman in a game in which fitness and your physical condition is so important. They began trying to stretch Brennan, looking at the areas where they felt he was most affected, and working out how they could help. They never said what they thought he might do. I don't know if that's because they didn't want to commit themselves; they said they thought that he could do this or that and there was a good chance of progress, but they never gave us false hopes. That was something they steered well away from, which impressed me. It's easy to latch onto things, we've done that before at places where they promised us what Brennan would do, and then we've been disheartened. We spoke to other families at the centre in Germany, who confirmed that the treatment for their children had worked. They were right and it's worked for Brennan, in fact it's been the only treatment he's had so far which has really made a difference. Even his speech has come on, he has become more alert and his appetite has improved.

At the beginning, they were doing the exercises for him, so it was really slow and I think they were disappointed. They didn't say anything, but that's the impression that came across. Erika wasn't

I always enjoy derbies against Leeds especially when I'm not on the receiving end.   ©RLphotos.com

Me and my two lads, Brennan and Fletcher, after another sleepless night.

Playing in the Federation Shield Final victory over Tonga.

Brennan beaming with my player of the year trophy in 2006 (proud of his dad).

Kicking a goal for England against France where I picked up the Man of the Match award.

Me and my two Wakefield team-mates, Brett Ferres and Ryan Atkins with the Federation Shield after beating Tonga. ©RLphotos.com

Directing play against Salford at the Willows. ©RLphotos.com

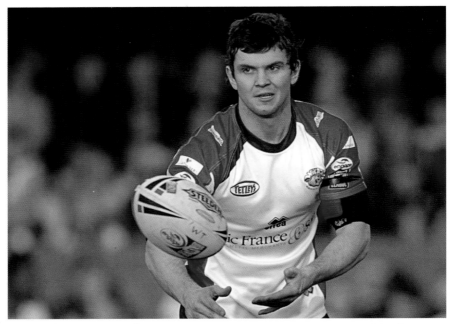

Feeding the support at Belle Vue.   *©RLphotos.com*

Taking one of my many shots at goal at Belle Vue.
©RLphotos.com

Tidying things up at the back in a Challenge Cup game against Bradford in 2007.
©*RLphotos.com*

Me, Erika, Brennan and Fletcher having a well earned rest on holiday in Tenerife in 2007.

Erika and Brennan on the beach in Tenerife.

Me and Fletcher enjoying the pool in Tenerife.

Brennan working hard with his physio, Tomasz, in Germany.

Brennan showing off to his mum and dad in Germany as he stood up for the first time.

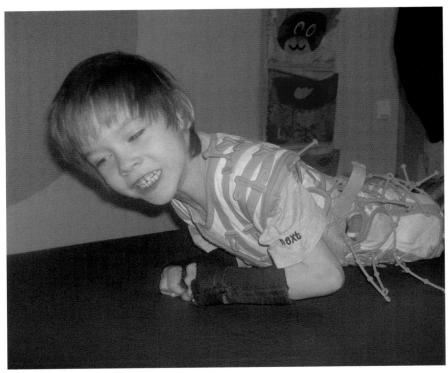

Brennan enjoying the work in Germany.

Diving past Paul White for the first try against Salford in 2008 in a Challenge Cup match. We went on to reach the semi-finals. ©RLphotos.com

dismayed at all, she came from the opposite direction and she could see quite clearly that Brennan was doing things that he hadn't done before, that he hadn't even been close to attempting in some instances, so she was naturally delighted. She'd known full well, right from the start, that it would be slow. She knew her son so well and realised it would take a fair while for Tomasz to get to know Brennan. Bren's like that; he has to trust someone first before he'll even begin to co-operate. Erika reckoned that's why he was crying all the time in the first few difficult weeks—he didn't feel at all comfortable with Tomasz, but after six or seven weeks, he was as happy as Larry to go in with him alone. Erika didn't leave the centre, she wouldn't have wanted to go away entirely, but she sat outside in reception, out of the way but reasonably close at hand, and he was fine. Then they'd shout her in from time to time so she could watch what they were doing. Initially they did all the stretches for him and showed him the patterns to do, but after a few weeks that turned around, and Brennan helped them.

There was a big breakthrough when he got a good step, so Erika could walk with him, holding his hand. That was a massive development. Previously he had been tight, walked jerkily and had not co-ordinated very well with a lot of involuntary movements. That's something they worked hard on to eradicate, or at least improve upon. We were also delighted that he'd calmed down, he didn't scream half as much, and his sleeping picked up. There was a marked improvement in every aspect, to an almost unbelievable extent.

The thing that stood out to Erika more than anything, and which impressed her very much, was Tomasz's patience and professionalism. He never lost his temper through all those hours of interminable screaming. He never shouted and then, once he'd gained Brennan's trust, if he kicked off he'd say, 'Right, lay him on the floor,' and would leave the room until Brennan shouted for him. To make it clear that he wasn't just responding to Brennan screaming, he waited until Brennan called his name. That taught us how to cope with his temper, which can be fierce to be frank. We got a good feeling from them and we were starting to realise that we would be alright.

Through everything, Brennan tried—and continues to try—his best. We knew that the first month would be the hardest for him, the most testing and probably the most traumatic, because everywhere we've taken him he's been the same; a bit withdrawn during the first week or two. But he's a trier, a gutsy lad, and we were quietly confident that once we got into it he'd do really well. They say at school that he pushes himself all the time; he's a courageous lad with a strong character. Because he loves being around other kids, it's good that we took Fletcher over. Brennan understands a lot more now. Erika keeps him totally informed, to help him get better. Every step of the way, she explains the process and he understands what's going on, and I'm sure he appreciates what the centre has done for him.

You really couldn't ask for anything better at the centre, it was very relaxed, they were patient, and they knew what was achievable and what wasn't. There were no high hopes, and therefore there were no disappointments. For Tomasz and Katarzyna, it's not just a job. Even after treatment, if Brennan wanted to play, Tomasz would stay with him. Their hearts were, and are, in it. Of the other centres we've been to, other than Brainwaves, of which we can't say anything negative, the attitude seemed to be, 'This is what you've got to do', the approach tended to be really strict in regimes that often operated six-hour days. Erika was under so much pressure to get things done. Tomasz, by contrast, simply says, 'Just do what you can do', while explaining in his own quiet understated way that the more we do, the more Brennan will come on. Erika appreciates that so much depends on what she can do, although not to the point of stressing herself out, and Tomasz suggested that we could take things with us to the park, so that exercises aren't always done in the house. He talked about trying to integrate them into everyday life, instead of having three-hour physio sessions, once he'd pointed that out to us it made a lot of sense. Erika did find this approach to be a lot easier.

There's always been a lot of equipment used with any other treatments we've been involved with. Brennan's had to go 'in there', or in a standing frame—which Tomasz and Katarzyna agree is good—or on a corner chair. But corner chairs can quite easily be moved elsewhere, and taken round to friends' and family's houses at home in England. Their view is that physiotherapy should come first, and equipment comes afterwards. In this country, it's the other way round. Things often look nice and impressive, but we've found in general that there's less effort to improve the children's skills. In Poland, they have the right priorities in our opinion. They settle for basic equipment and, having cut costs in that regard, spend more money on therapy. Here in England, therapy tends to get forgotten while we get the best equipment.

It's not just the therapy, either, it's the whole approach. There were constant reminders, made in the right way, from them that we had to remember why we had brought Brennan to Germany in the first place; that he would have a better life if the treatment worked. They said this in such a way that it never gave us any false hope. We were told that lots of children react in the same way to begin with and that Brennan wasn't crying through pain but through frustration, simply because the exercises were really hard for him to do—but that, over the months, it would become easier for him. That's exactly how it worked out, we were delighted to find. It wasn't easy though. The thing with Brennan is that he is quite stubborn, and when he says 'No' he means it. There's no messing from him. Tomasz said we had to keep pushing him and not give in to his cries as he would win (and ultimately lose) if we backed down. He had to know that he had to do all the exercises, no picking and choosing. Brennan had ones he liked, which he tried hard at, and ones he hated, that he screamed and protested at and tried to get away from. But they had to carry on through this, which was a dreadful experience, and Erika couldn't step in to 'help' him, which she found hard. In order to get the best results she had to stand by and simply watch.

Tomasz and Katarzyna were fantastic they really couldn't do enough for us. They tried to make Brennan's exercises fun, in the way that rugby league coaches will attempt to make training more enjoyable I suppose, so that players don't necessarily realise how much they're doing. As I said in an earlier chapter, in the first week Brennan got an ear infection, necessitating a trip to the doctor, and about eight weeks into the treatment Erika incurred a bad water and kidney infection, which meant another visit to the medics. Katarzyna and Tomasz were very helpful and took them to the doctors. When we had a problem or two in the apartment they came straight round and fixed those for us. There was no 'nine-to-five' attitude, they were like friends and when I went over we went out with them for a nice, relaxed meal. The feeling we have, from Germany, is very positive. What a difference there was on our return from the first trip, when Erika took Brennan to Pontefract hospital. The reaction from the paediatrician was that there was still only minimal movement in Brennan's right arm, and that he couldn't get the full range of movement in his right leg. And she started to talk about tube feeding yet again. We came from a high in Germany, went to Pontefract, and got flattened.

Brennan put a bit of weight on while we were over there, where they gave us hope that he can have a good life. Back home, by contrast, everything is always so negative from the medics, where their idea seems to be that everyone should be treated exactly the same way regardless of their individual condition. They take no note of personal circumstances, it seems to me. In Germany, they told us that there is no way Brennan should have a tube inserted in his stomach. In their view that would make him more disabled. They advised us that we should try everything else before tube feeding, and that it should be a last resort and nothing more. We go with their opinion, our decision is based on the progress Brennan's made. He started, after a while, to take well to Tomasz and Ola and not scream and shout half as much. Tomasz is a tall man and whenever he held Bren he reminded Erika of a friendly giant. He was always so patient with him, he never raised his voice and he always tried to make it all light-hearted and fun. He has many years of experience with disabled children and it shows.

We don't like to think too much about how far Brennan will progress. Everyone's different, and we don't want to raise our hopes and come crashing back down to earth—because that would finish us off. We just wanted, when we went to Germany, to get him to sit up on his own, to help him develop and give him some independence.

Anything else was a bonus. It's a rugby league cliché, I know, but we really do just take it week by week. If we look any further than that, we're setting ourselves up for a fall. We've had a few of those over the past five years, and we're not sure after those experiences whether we'd be able to handle any more. Some days Brennan shows improvement and, in the end, that's good enough for us. He's trying his hardest, he always has done and that's all we can ask of him. Sticking my neck out, though, I do think it will work eventually, it will just take time. It's a bit like trying to improve a team or a player—you can't build a side overnight. It was the same with Brennan's treatment—we've got to be patient and keep positive for him.

I had a taste of that in rugby league terms when I was called back into the side for the match with Leeds. This was at a stage when Brennan's treatment wasn't going so well, he was still finding himself in Germany, and it had been a tough week for Erika and the kids. Then I got a late call-up into the team. I think Tevita Leo-Latu had pulled out the day before. I was on the bench in a strange game that I'd forget if possible. We were 38–0 down when I was introduced in the second half, but had the better of the second period. I enjoyed being back out there with the lads, although the result wasn't the best we've ever had. At least it got the rustiness out of me. From a personal perspective we 'won' the second half, after I came on, but a lot of factors can come into that. It's possible of course that Leeds eased off. I'd like to think that I made some sort of difference, and I felt part of things again. There was more good news for the club as well. We were progressing in the Carnegie Challenge Cup and became increasingly talked about as a side that could make an impact, particularly with the canny John Kear at the helm.

John knows more than most about what it takes to succeed in the competition, having won the trophy with Sheffield in 1998 and with Hull in 2006. We'd overcome a potentially difficult first hurdle with what turned out to be a fairly comfortable victory at Salford, who were in the Co-operative National League One but had remained full time. That had been followed by a win at Barrow, where we had prevailed in 1963—the last time we had lifted the Challenge Cup, which was seen by some folk as an omen. So the fates appeared to be conspiring in our favour, and a home draw with Oldham—once one of the game's great sides but now languishing in National League 2—suggested to the optimistic among our fans that perhaps something special was brewing.

Hearteningly, we were beginning to show welcome and solid signs of the kind of resilience that takes a team to Wembley. There was a strong indication of this in a stirring 18–16 Super League victory at Huddersfield, achieved despite a crippling injury list. It was a day when young players rose magnificently to the occasion, and on which the gnarled old veterans reacted positively to having the new kids on the block alongside them. Having youngsters around the place brings the best out of the older players. If you can get the right mix of youth and experience then you're going to have a good side, and I think that's what happened against Huddersfield. We went in as underdogs, with no pressure on us, in fact I don't think I've ever played in a winning side against the Giants which, given that they are not quite seen as one of the leading sides, more a solid mid-table team, is a strange statistic.

No one outside Belle Vue particularly expected us to win, so everyone was relaxed. All the kids played well, at or around the top of their individual games. I think that lifted the older players, and it showed in our performance. The Giants could have played for a week and I don't think they'd have scored another try after we kept them at bay in the second half. Our defence was brilliant on that particular afternoon. In Super League these days it doesn't matter who the 17 are, if the opposition doesn't turn up to play, you're going to beat them. That's what happened, I'd guess. Huddersfield looked at our team, with 11 first teamers out, including Adam Watene, who had to return home to New Zealand following the death of his father, and with four or five teenagers playing in their stead, and thought, 'This will be easy'. We surprised them. We got the two points in one of the best victories I've been involved in with the Wakefield Trinity Wildcats. With the side we had playing, it was a massive achievement, a real stunner and hopefully a pointer to the future. The bookies gave us a 14 points start, which says it all because they're no mugs, and if any one of our players had doubted that we could have won, I don't believe we would have done. But we had trained well all week and everyone believed we could win. It spurred us on that they'd beaten us four times the previous year, which had cost us a place in the play-offs and was a hard pill to swallow at the time. It shows clearly that if players stick together and abide by the game plan, anything is possible. The young players deserve a lot of credit for the win, they seemed to come in without any fear and John Kear should get plenty of praise for having faith in them. It was a lesson in how to rise above adversity, which Erika and I know something about, and it was a reminder also that much of the game is played in the mind. You can train the house down all week, but if you're sitting in the changing room with your mind on something else, or you're thinking it's going to be easy, then all that hard work will just have been a waste of time. You've got to have the right mental approach as well, that's vital, and in some ways I think that's a bigger factor than the physical aspect. If you've got the mentality right, then I'm sure you're going to win more games than you're going to lose.

Everyone wrote us off, but John loves being the underdog. He's been in that role so many times in the Challenge Cup, he knows how to handle the situation. He'd rather have that position; there's no pressure, no one expects you to win, and if you do lose no one is going to bag you. If you manage to win, though, they'll all stand up and take note, and I think that's what we did against the Giants. I never got the chance to speak to Jon Sharp afterwards, who lost his job only a couple of months later despite having his contract extended. I felt very sorry when that news came through and if I'd had any inkling that it was on the horizon— but of course I wasn't to know—maybe I'd have sought him out. He'd probably gone into a corner, like Jon does. That's sport isn't it? When you win you don't want to go around shouting your mouth off, and I wouldn't have wanted to go in gloating or anything like that.

Obviously when I bump into him, I have a chat, but it's fair to say that on that day he'd have been balled off with the result and he'd have wanted to get out as quickly as he could. I didn't want to be the one to ring him up the next day and start on about the match. They'd given us enough pastings over the years, and somehow the victory made us start to think that maybe this year could be our year, especially with Brad Drew and Paul Reilly around. Neither player was fit for the Huddersfield game but, having both been with the Giants for a number of years, the information they were able to pass on about their old team was invaluable. They were a perfect illustration of the value to a club of players who take a positive attitude despite, for whatever reason, not being out there on the park.

The victory set us up nicely for what looked for all the world like being a testing trip to Salford City Reds in the fourth round of the Carnegie Challenge Cup. In some ways, it was a daunting pairing, Salford having remained full time following relegation from Super League the previous season, and John Kear—ever the perfectionist—was taking no chances whatsoever. The detailed video review he took us through in the build-up to the game was probably the most intense session we've ever done on the opposition, of any standard, during my time at Wakefield, which shows how seriously John takes the competition. Nigel Wright, one of Trinity's truly great former players and now back at Belle Vue as Under 21s coach told us that when he was at Wigan, they had won something like 40-odd Challenge Cup games on the trot. The Challenge Cup was almost stuck to the boardroom table at Central Park. Then they went to Salford and got turned over in one of the most unexpected results of recent years. The result had shattered all the Wigan players. He rammed home the message that we didn't need reminding that we had to avoid sitting there next week doing the same, and ruminating over what had gone wrong. Everyone at the club was looking for a good run in the competition and I was as keen as anyone. I don't think I've ever been past the fifth round and that was a record I wanted to get rid of.

Nigel said, by way of explanation, that Wigan turned up for the tie with Salford in a casual way, thinking that it was going to be easy, a cakewalk. They were as good as in the next round, that was the general opinion—and not one only held at Central Park, it had to be said—and everything in training was light-hearted. They got their comeuppance by going out in one of the biggest upsets in recent Challenge Cup history. His talk was timely; it gave us all a real kick up the backside and it reminded us all that we had to be prepared for a tough game, because Salford were still full time players. We had to be on our guard because they would want to prove, as a club, as a team and as individual players, that they were still good enough for Super League. And they'd leave no stone unturned in the attempt.

It was a proper 'banana skin' of a tie and not one of us wanted to be reflecting the following week on, 'I wish I'd done this better' or 'I wish I'd done that differently'. We went to the Willows fully prepared; we were not taking the game lightly, not by any stretch of the imagination, and the extensive video review was invaluable. We always look at film of the opposition, but we know a lot about so many of the players in Super League anyway. Salford were more of an unknown quantity and needed a different and more intense approach because of that. John, as a coach, understood that and made sure that we had the benefit of an in-depth briefing on each and every player in their side. He was also able to get inside Salford's heads, in the sense that they were the underdogs and he knew, having been in that situation so often himself previously, what they would be saying in the build-up to the game. He's good at things like that and we were fully prepared for the match. The fact that it was televised gave our opponents a bigger incentive to beat us, on the national stage and under the glare of the spotlight.

We were keen to progress, and for all that we were taking Salford very seriously, the fact remained that we'd been given a good draw, which is a handy thing at every stage of the Challenge Cup and isn't to be wasted. Teams need good draws up to the quarter finals, which is often a one-off game. Most years, if you get one of the top sides at that stage, and they're not on the ball that day, then you can beat them and you're in the semi-final—and before you know it you're suddenly in the final. 'What better feeling can there be than walking out at Wembley?' were my thoughts in the build-up to the Salford tie. That really would be the highlight of my career.

In the end we maybe needn't have worried too much—or perhaps the fact that we did natter about the match was a key factor in our 38–8 victory. It sounds comfortable enough, and I suppose in the end it was, but Salford gave us a tough test and we certainly struggled in the opening quarter before establishing a 22–8 interval lead and pulling away in the second period. My try in the 20th minute set the tone for touchdowns by centres Ryan Atkins and Scott Grix within the next six minutes and Salford never recovered, despite hooker Malcolm Alker's touchdown a few seconds before the interval shortly after our hooker Sam Obst had bustled over. Unanswered tries in the second half from scrum half Danny Brough (who totalled five goals), winger Sean Gleeson and substitute Tevita Leo-Latu perhaps confirmed our superiority on the day.

All that mattered at one time in rugby league was the Challenge Cup and Wembley, older fans tell me. The league used to be almost a side issue in those days. Things have changed in that regard since the launch of Super League, and obviously I want to get into the play-offs. But I think I'd swap that for a Challenge Cup Final. The competition means a lot to players, very few end their careers having played in a final. Before I bring the curtain down on my own career I want to have featured in a final of some sort. Where better than Wembley?

John Kear knows all about winning Challenge Cup Finals, and the Wildcats have a fine pedigree, going back to the 1960s, when Wakefield Trinity were the glamour team and played at Wembley on four occasions. The fact that Trinity have a glorious history isn't mentioned too much. We all know that we last won it in 1963, and when John's talking about the Challenge Cup you can see a real buzz in him, he fairly fizzes. It's obvious he loves the competition to bits and that inevitably feeds into the players. Our feeling, as we embarked on the competition, was that if we could get into the quarter finals we'd probably be the underdogs. John knows about that role and, who knows, if we could just work our way through to that stage, anything could happen. Then it would be the semi-final, at a neutral venue, and by then it's simply about what happens on the day. Anybody can beat anybody. If you can't get up for that then you'll never get up for anything. In the Super League Grand Final, you've got to qualify for the play-offs and then beat everyone else—but the top sides get two bites, so it's not about one game. But in the Challenge Cup, it's a massive feeling to get to the final. Wakefield were picking up at the right time.

Neil Fox, who played in three of Trinity's four finals in the 1960s, is around the place of course, but he doesn't talk about it much, he's not one to blow his own trumpet. We had enough in the squad—Danny Brough's played in a Challenge Cup Final, for Hull, plus John—who knew what it was all about, and they both said that it was the best feeling they had in their entire careers, and that they wanted it again. The rest of us wanted to taste it for the first time. Meanwhile, we were mooted seriously as a top six team by the media in general. That's how it is in Super League. There's no relegation obviously, but you only need a couple of wins to be discussed in those terms. Everything is black or white. Suffer two losses, you're favourites for the drop—or would be if relegation still existed—but notch a couple of wins and you're favourites for the top six. That's how close it's getting. I said in 2007, all along, that we set off too well and faded away towards the business end. In 2008 it seemed to have reversed, we opened slowly but as the season went on we gradually picked up. The hope was that by round 17 and 18 we'd reach our peak and have a better chance of making the top six. Picking up wins along the way when not playing at our best would be an added bonus.

Not that teams don't go out trying to win every game, the attitude of structuring a season is more in terms of performance than results. We want to win all our games, of course we do, and barring the Leeds fixture at home we'd been in with a shout as the Challenge Cup campaign beckoned in just about every match. In the first four or five games of the season, we just missed out, but suddenly we'd started to get the results we wanted.

It's striking how Trinity's improvement in the 2008 season coincided with Brennan's progress in Germany. His improvement was all down to his own grit and determination, of course, plus the hard work of Tomasz and Katarzyna, and Erika's love, but somehow things seem to be fated. I like to think that videos of us winning games didn't exactly hinder his development, and Erika said that he really enjoyed watching them, although he cried if we lost. She asks him to cross his fingers for Daddy before matches, and he does it. If I'm taking a shot at goal he says, 'Plea...se' and when I score he goes, 'Ye...s.' If I miss, it's, 'Oo...oh.' Not that I ever miss!

The family all helped in Germany, with my mam going over for a week to give Erika's mam, Lynn, a deserved break. Understandably they'd started to get on each other's nerves, but Lynn had been brilliant, she'd left her husband behind for so long and it must have been hard on her. Everyone was thinking the same, that everything possible must be done to help Brennan, his future is paramount. The experience brought home to Erika how precious her mam is to her, she simply couldn't have gone to Germany, aiming for a better life for Brennan, without her. When Erika found out that Bren was ill Lynn gave up her job to be there for us, and she always has been there. Erika, rightly, considers herself very lucky to have Lynn as her mother.

We all had a further boost when they put him in a specially adapted suit, the Therasuit. They said he would be very tired afterwards and that it would be hard for him, but he seemed to love it and when Erika took him into the centre each morning he would shout out, 'Tomasz suit'. He looked so cute in it and used to laugh when they put it on. Brennan also has a 'sleep system' to use every night, which was developed in England and which Erika took to Germany with her. It's essentially a foam mattress that keeps him straight, because he gets twisted, and it's got pumice between his legs to keep his hips in line, because he has to be symmetrical and remain in a good position. We brought it back to England after the first period of treatment. The hope was that, after using the Therasuit, he'd be tired each night and that the system would help him sleep properly.

There were some good days, such as the morning Brennan worked especially hard at all the exercises and never cried once. They asked Erika to help with his walking on that occasion, as he was shouting for her, and he did so well, doing better than ever with her assistance. She had really wanted to be part of it and it gave her a huge lift. Tomasz called Brennan a champion at the end of that session, and Bren loved that. Ola told us we were on the right track and Erika knew then that we had made the correct decision. She felt so positive and couldn't wait to ring everyone and tell them how well he had done. She worked on him when they returned home, before going back, giving him an hour of therapy before going to work. When he went to school, they put him in his walker and in his standing frame, and when Erika got home she'd give him another hour, then he went in the corner chair again at night. We were managing to do it, but it was difficult. Erika doesn't like to push it too hard, because Brennan can become unhappy when she gets stressed when—like anyone else—she can get snappy. She also wanted him to enjoy his time at home as much as he possibly could before going back to Germany. It had become clear that a factor in the success in Germany was that Tomasz tried to make everything fun for Brennan, and that was something we wanted to abide by.

Through Tomasz, Brennan has picked up patterns that will change his life. Previously, when dressing, he would always be tight, and we would have to force his arms into his sleeves. After two or three months in Germany, he'd started to put his arms out, enabling us to put his coat on. Everyday things like that are starting to make such a difference. When they went to the Chinese restaurant in Ratingen he fed himself with a small fork. He was happy, sitting there, just stabbing at his food, trying to eat it himself. And there was a massive development when he sat on a chair on his own, without any real support other than the

Therasuit. Erika was sat in reception at the centre, and Tomasz shouted her in. There Brennan was, perched on a little stool. We'd been waiting for that for years. As Erika said, that was incredible progress and it simply wouldn't have happened if we hadn't gone to Germany. I noticed when I went over, without Erika having to point anything out to me, that Brennan's arms and legs seemed to be much looser. He was holding his arms much lower, nearer to his knees, and his hands were open. He no longer had his fists clenched. It was a fantastic sight.

11

DEDICATION

There was a suggestion, when relegation from Super League was removed from the equation at the beginning of the 2008 season, that some teams could perhaps drift into the comfort zone. Whispers here and there that clubs without a realistic hope of challenging for the title, or making a serious bid for the top six, could be tempted to cut back on team strengthening in the knowledge that they would remain in the top flight anyhow. I'd heard those rumours myself but if there was any substance in them there was no sign of it at Belle Vue. Things have improved steadily, dramatically almost, in the six years I've been at Wakefield. It wasn't too good in my early days at Trinity. We didn't have a conditioner, and we had to do things like fetch our own drinks.

Everything has improved since then. John Kear has been a good coach and the club seems to be heading the right way. Since his arrival, the club has become more professional than anything I'd seen previously in my time at Wakefield, and it's a good place to be. I hope that the club can go further. There seems to be positive news, although it can often be hazy, about a new stadium, and you never know where we'll be in the next two or three years if we get the ground up and running.

In the 2008 season we seemed, apart from a poor run after qualifying for the Challenge Cup semi-final, to have picked up a habit of winning close games. This is a great attribute to have, both as individual players and as a collective unit. That raises the question of whether results of that type arise from sheer match-winning ability, or because of mental strength, or whether it's just how it's gone. I think it's largely a matter of just how it's gone. Previously when we lost it would invariably have been down to the bounce of the ball, or because of a one-off penalty, or a missed one-on-one tackle. It's not as though it was usually a team issue when we lost a few games at the beginning of this year, individual errors cost us. This is not as big a deal as when it's a team problem. Things happen in rugby: you can slip in a tackle, get your feet wrong, or simply lose the ball. But our team performances were good. We seemed to be playing better every game, Danny Brough and I gelled better than we had previously. Everybody seems to be picking up at the right time.

If we could keep doing that then we'd be in with a real shout at the end of the season (so would every other club in Super League). At the end of the season I planned to join Erika, Brennan and Fletcher in Germany, stay there for a good while, and give Erika's mum a break. I was looking forward to that, obviously, it would be good to have a full two months or so with them. On the other hand, I didn't want the season to end too early, in fact I would have been delighted if we could have forced our way through to the Grand Final. And, at the end of the day, why shouldn't we? If we got into the play-offs, who knows what would transpire? The top six was our definite aim, there would be no point playing otherwise. It's getting harder in Super League, everyone improves season by season. It's no longer the case that just one or two sides can get into the play-offs and win it any more. That number has expanded to five or six and made it a good competition.

The fact that there is no relegation isn't a factor in the dressing room, and I don't recall it even being discussed. Super League is as strong as it's ever been, in fact stronger I'd say, and every team wants to avoid finishing bottom, whether there's relegation or not. There's no notion that, because there's no relegation, we're not bothered. It just doesn't happen like that, we still want to win, and we still want to get into finals. It's been put to me that the absence of relegation can remove anxiety, because it's no longer an absolute disaster to finish bottom of the pile. I don't really go along with that either. Maybe with three or four games to go, if you can't make the play-offs any more you'd start to think, well we can't get relegated. You could start thinking like that, yes, but until that point arrives you would definitely focus on making the play-offs. We would at Wakefield, at any rate, I suppose I can't speak properly for others. Nobody in the game wants players to think, 'There's no relegation, so we're not bothered.' Everyone, as a professional, focuses on looking upwards, towards the top six. We made the play-offs once in my time at Wakefield, when I was injured, having damaged my knee. We beat Hull at Hull, and then lost at Wigan. It's a tough call, when you come in at six, having to play away all the time, but in a sense, once you've made the six, the pressure's off. You're playing away, so no one expects you to win, and most players seem to perform a lot better when little is expected of them.

I think that's what we did in 2004. We hadn't beaten Hull in three or four outings when we travelled to the east coast, but we went there and turned them over. Rugby is a funny old game, it doesn't always work in the favourite's way. Leeds were the form team of early 2008 and took some beating but I fully expected them to have a dip in form at some stage, which did indeed happen when they lost at Castleford, although that seemed to spur them on a bit more. I saw that game and people said the Tigers only won because Leeds were poor but, for me, the Tigers played well. They still had to score tries. If you don't prepare as if you're going into a Cup Final, you will get beaten in Super League. Leeds, to my mind, eased off a bit after winning the World Club Challenge with a dramatic victory over Melbourne Storm. There was a mental thing involved. Playing in the World Club Challenge one week at Elland Road and then going to Castleford appeared to affect some Leeds players. Deep inside some of them seemed to think they only had to turn up to win. If you play with that attitude, you're going to lose. That's how it is—one week you are seeing off the top sides, the next you are losing to the so-called strugglers.

There's a view that the right approach is to try to convince yourself that the opposition is very slightly better than you are. At Wakefield, over the last few years, we've always tended to play well against the top sides. When we take on teams around us, we don't always perform as well. It's as though when you go into battle, you rise to the occasion. Jason Demetriou is a player who always does just that. His 2008 season was hit by injury and we missed him. He leads by example and maybe that's one reason he was shifted into the pack at the beginning of the season. I can see the logic behind that. But I think there is also an argument against it. If he's in the middle of the park it can reduce his impact; one of his strengths is coming in and out of the game. In the middle of the park he's in the game all the time, and that does inevitably tire him out. I did prefer it, personally, when he was in the centre, because he did manage to make a lot of line breaks. He's put a bit of weight on because he knew he would be playing in the pack this year. But wherever he plays, you'll always get 110 per cent from him, and that's what John Kear wants.

John is understanding and sympathetic over the situation with Brennan and my family. One of his big plusses as a coach is his man-management and if he dropped me on my form, I'd accept that. In fact I wouldn't like to be played just because my family's away in Germany and because he's feeling sorry for me. It's a team sport at the end of the day and we have to climb that ladder as much as any of the other sides. The job of coaches is to get players to be as good as they can be in every way, including mentally, and the situation with my family is obviously a mental rather than a physical thing. I'm sure, on reflection, that John's considered all the ins and outs and reflected on how he can get the best out of me in a difficult period. He keeps asking how things are, and he's stressed that the door's always open for me to go and have a chat. I'm not one of those people to be open with my emotions, though, I tend to bottle it all up.

John Kear's one of the best coaches I've had, and I've had some good ones. There were so many at Featherstone. I made my first team league debut for Kevin Hobbs, who quit after his family was abused by a section of Rovers' support after a defeat at struggling Doncaster. Then, I think, Simon Tuffs stepped up on a caretaker basis (I don't reckon many fans would be silly enough to abuse him) and he was in charge for three weeks. I think we did pretty well under him. I didn't get to see him much, but he did coach me for a while in the Under 21s. It's said that his man-management skills aren't the best, but that's Tuffsy for you. You get what you see with him—if you're not performing, he'll let you know. That's how he is, he's not bothered who he upsets. Then I think Peter Roe and Ian Fairhurst were my next coaches. Peter was a big plus for my career as he nursed me into it. He didn't play me at all at the start of the season, then his half back got injured so he had to shove me back in quicker than he'd thought. That was the year I went on to be the Young Player of the Year. Peter always looked out for me. He was good with the press, always putting my name forward for international honours, so he did a lot for me. I still speak to him every now and again. Before him, Andy Kelly coached, he was another good man-manager. John Kear ranks with any coach I've ever come across, though, and he guided us superbly in our Challenge Cup run, which seemed to run nicely in tandem with Brennan's notable progress.

Erika phoned me in tears when he sat up in Germany unaided, she said it was the best thing she's ever witnessed. That was very pleasing, and I felt even better when I saw it for myself when I went over. He sat up talking to us, and I'd never seen that before in my life. It brought a tear to my eye. He loved it. He sat supported in a chair with his feet just off the floor. They'd positioned him, with something underneath his feet. At first, when he realised that no one was holding him, he started to panic, but he eventually became used to it and wanted to do it more. He's making real progress now; I think that, because he'd never done it before, he got scared. It was something new to him, like riding a bike. It's scary when first in the saddle but after a few times it doesn't bother you, and it's the same with him. The physio says he can do things, the only issue is that he has to be trained to do it, because he's being asked to do things which he's never done before. They've had him walking, holding his hand as he's gone down the corridor. At first he was anxious about it but now he loves doing it, he wants to do it all the time.

At the moment there's always someone holding his hands and keeping him balanced, but he's got his legs moving properly now. It's amazing what they've done in the short time he's been there. God knows what he's going to be like after two years. It's phenomenal, a dream come true for us, we never thought we'd see him sitting up. His speech and everything has improved, and we can hardly believe it.

We never had any serious doubts about taking Brennan to Germany other than concerns we had in the first few weeks when he was unsettled, although we never really knew what we were going to achieve through it. With everything we'd been through, we didn't want to get our hopes up too much, we just took it day by day, in the same way as players and coaches will talk about taking it 'match by match' I suppose. To be fair, I don't think we expected much but after seeing the results after three months, it's been amazing. As the physio says, Brennan loves doing things he's used to doing; when he has to do something different he's not so keen, but once he's started to do it, and started to enjoy it, he wants to do it more. He's possibly like me. I wouldn't fancy playing at prop at first with the big misters running at me. But the more you do it, the more you get used to it, although I think that applies more to Brennan going through his exercises and routines than me switching to the front row. Seriously, though, Erika and I are pleased with how it's going and although it's been hard we can't wait to get him over there again to resume his treatment.

It's weird, when we first set out on the course of treatment I was petrified, I didn't like being apart from my family. Now we just can't wait to return to Germany for some more good results. It's a strange feeling really, but if we'd been there for three months and not seen any results, we wouldn't feel so excited, obviously, about returning.

I'd go so far as to say we don't want to stop. I wouldn't say we're enjoying it, it's been pretty hard on Erika. She's had nothing different to do, just doing the same things every day, and she deserves a lot of credit for still having a smile on her face. Just seeing Brennan doing things that we never thought he'd do has helped her a lot more. When I visited last time she said she couldn't wait to get back to England but these days, once she's back home, she can't wait to return to Germany to see Brennan improve more. When she's not here it sometimes feels as though she is, as she checks up on me via the web cam. It's usually a case of, 'Are the builders doing this properly? Are they doing that? I don't like that there.' So she might as well be at home. She's a fantastic lady and what she's doing for Brennan is terrific. I go out there for a couple of days and being one of those who has to be doing something all the time I start to puff and blow. She's been out there for three months and she's still cracking jokes. Seeing Brennan sit up has given her a real boost. It looks like he's showing off in the pictures, even I couldn't believe it.

My reaction when Erika rang with the news that Brennan had sat up is hard to describe. I was on something of a roller coaster ride anyway while she was away; up one minute, down the next. That news did perk me up for a week or two. And when I went over and saw it for myself, it gave me a real lift.

In sport, as well, one week you're up, the next you're down. Things just seem to be coming together on both fronts. When I'm feeling down about Brennan, my rugby's down. When I start hearing good news about him, my rugby picks up. People will say that I've been handling it okay, but looking at my performances, it does have an effect on me when things aren't going so well for Brennan. Hopefully my rugby will go through the roof again and I'll start to hit a bit of form. If he can keep picking up like he has been doing, I'll probably get the Man of Steel at the end of next year. Family does have an effect on me; I didn't think, however, that the effect would be as great as it has been.

Beyond my family and me, Wakefield are rising. These things don't happen overnight, they take time, but it's coming together now. We're not known as a bottom two side anymore and we'll always be challenging for the play-offs. John Kear has had a lot to do with that. He's not just focussed on his job, he's thinking about the future of the club, and bringing through young kids. He pays a lot of attention to the Academy and Under 21s sides, and I think he'll be at Wakefield for a long time. The effect of all this is that the atmosphere at Wakefield has been good for the last few seasons, people have started to get behind us and crowds have been steadily building. They were up last year and I'm sure they will be bigger this year. There's a good feeling about the place and I enjoy playing for the club.

One thing I really do like is the playing surface at Belle Vue which is one of the best in Super League. The groundsman, Bathy as we call him, looks after it as if it's his child. I know the ground itself isn't everyone's favourite but as players we're not really bothered what's around the field so long as the playing surface is okay. The new stadium is out of our hands, and we haven't talked about it. But it would be a crying shame, a disaster really, if we don't get it, because we'd be out of Super League. The issue needs resolving soon. Beyond the players' perspective, although there isn't a better playing surface in the game, the terracing surrounds are old now, and we do need to move as soon as possible. When the ground's full, the atmosphere at Belle Vue is great, but it can slip a little when the crowd is thinner. There have been some good crowds as people are starting to come to watch us. When we play teams like Catalans and London we see how well the crowds are bearing up, because on those days only our supporters come to the game.

The fans have been great to me, and so has everyone within the club; the players, the coaching staff, especially John Kear who takes a wider view about everything. Not that I need particular motivation. I enjoy training and learning and there's always something new to pick up. I gained a lot from the GB camp in late 2007, for example, and even on my holidays I get up early and do a bit because, to me, the game is about dedication. The more dedicated you are, the longer your career is likely to last, barring serious injury. Erika thinks I'll play until I'm 40, but I'm not so sure I'll last that long. Brad Davis didn't get far off that mark— he looked after himself well—but you have to keep yourself fit. I think nowadays people tend to retire just because everyone else is retiring, but if my body's feeling well when I'm 36, and if I'm still doing the business, I'll carry on playing. After that, I don't know. I don't think I'll get involved in physiotherapy when I retire as a player. Tommy Smales, when he was playing, always used to treat himself; it was something he'd always been interested in. It's not something I'd do, at this stage I don't know what I'll turn to when I retire.

12

SEMI-FINAL
SICKNESS

Have you heard of Wembleyitis? Well, we've conjured up another ailment at Wakefield Trinity Wildcats and it's not one I can honestly say I've ever heard of before. It's called semi-finalitis and we well and truly caught the bug after our Carnegie Challenge Cup quarter final victory over Oldham. Following that win the draw the next evening paired us with Hull FC, we carried on with a decent run, recording three successive victories. But then we seemed to hit a wall and could do little right. It was as if the possibility of appearing at Wembley overshadowed everything else to the point where we struggled to win a game. I'd better rephrase that. We didn't exactly struggle. The correct term is we failed, which explains precisely what happened in the couple of months or so between the win against Oldham and the semi-final with Hull at Doncaster.

That reference to the timescale between the games may go some way to explaining our alarming drop in form, but it's no excuse. As a player you have to take every match as it comes and, for a side with genuine top six aspirations, slipping to four successive defeats was unacceptable. That's certainly how John Kear saw it and he made his feelings plain—not merely regarding the reverses themselves, but their manner. Kear's man-management is superb but even he couldn't hide his frustration at setbacks against Catalans on our own patch at Warrington five days later when we shipped 60 points, at home to Hull, and at Bradford. It's a familiar syndrome in the competition but in the past it's generally been confined to the build-up to the final itself, when players have perhaps not performed at their best for fear of sustaining an injury that could have ruled them out of a Wembley appearance.

That's unacceptable, but I suppose we have to accept that rugby league players are only human and they cannot be blamed for worrying about missing out on a major occasion. It's different, to my mind, when you're only at the semi-final stage, although there are those who might argue that there is even more at stake in a way as the major 'prize' could be seen as appearing at Wembley rather than winning the Challenge Cup. I don't go along with that—there's no point playing in any game if you're not planning to win it—but I think I can understand the viewpoint. If there's something in it, and if our bout of semi-finalitis catches on, maybe the Rugby Football League should seriously consider playing the penultimate round no later than a fortnight after the quarter finals. That way teams, players—and coaches and fans for that matter—wouldn't have too long to fret about their future progress or otherwise in the Challenge Cup.

If I'm honest, I think it got to us as a collective unit. There's no other rational explanation. Consider the facts. We went into the quarter final against Oldham in ninth spot and firmly in contention for a top six berth. We backed up that victory with a stunning success at Castleford where three of us—all former Tigers and therefore perhaps with points to prove—crossed the whitewash. I took particular delight in my touchdown, Damien Blanch had extra reason for jubilation over his two tries and Danny Brough— well, Broughie just enjoys scoring, we all know that, and he had no complaints about totalling 16 points with a try and six goals. Wakefield added to the win at the Jungle—never the easiest of venues, as the Tigers proved in the same season when, despite occupying bottom spot, they beat Leeds and St Helens and drew with Wigan—by hosting Huddersfield and edging our old *bête noirs* in a high-scoring if torrid clash. A week later we were at Hull KR where our spirit was vividly illustrated with a 26–18 victory. Those of little faith wouldn't have put much money on our prospects, even with the best odds William Hill might have to offer, as the match headed to a close. The Robins, with only 17 minutes left, were 18–4 up and the doubters could have been forgiven for reckoning that we had little hope of victory.

Our self belief, though, was vividly illustrated by a sensational recovery which condemned Hull Kingston Rovers to a third successive defeat and helped propel us into the top four. Aussie Brad Drew set the agenda on his return off the bench, forcing his way over from short range and Brough goaling. Brough then sent centre Ryan Atkins in at the corner with a trademark long pass to level the scores, and I'm glad to say that I scored the try that levelled the issue. Winger Sean Gleeson and hooker Sam Obst did all the work prising open the Rovers defence, and all I had to do was fetch up on Obst's shoulder to cross by the posts, Brough edging us in front with his conversion. As if that wasn't enough, we closed in style when Drew danced over at the finish. But, after that victory, the wheels unaccountably fell off the wagon. The frustrating thing is that our next game, at home to Catalans Dragons, should on no account have ended in defeat. We played the match on a Tuesday evening, Catalans having supplied several of the players who had turned out for France against England in the 56–8 defeat at Toulouse four days previously. We were 10 points up within 12 minutes, courtesy of tries by Gleeson and Blanch, Brough kicking a conversion, and then it all went horribly wrong. Catalans pulled back to 14–10 at half time and, amazingly, it was one-way traffic in the second period as the Frenchmen eased to a demoralising 30–14 victory that should never have happened.

John Kear said: 'You would have thought half my team had been playing on Friday night, and not half the Catalans. We controlled the game for 30 minutes and then we were on the back foot for 50 minutes. It was the worst 40 minutes we've played for a long, long time and that's a worry.' Kear had more reason to be fretful after the next three games. Warrington put us to the sword the following weekend, piping

60 points into our pump at the Halliwell Jones Stadium, and we lost 26–18 at home to Hull in our next fixture after having led 12–6 at the break.

John Kear became frustrated and reflected: 'You've got to question our mental fortitude. The semi-final is coming up and you try not to let it affect you, but I think it obviously is. That's the stark reality of the situation. Our standards have dropped dramatically in the last three weeks; our form is very scratchy at the moment and it's the worst possible month for it. I'm sick of trotting out the same reasons. I don't know whether the problem is mental or physical, but there is obviously a problem. You only have to look at our last three second half performances.'

It was a similar story at Odsal in what, thankfully, was our last outing before the semi-final, Bradford Bulls overturning a 6–0 interval deficit—and the sin binning of Sam Burgess—to beat us 24–10. Kear, though, was in a more upbeat mood afterwards and said: 'I feel we made steps forward today and played better. We are thinking of next week now.'

We were also thinking of David Topliss, the former Trinity 'great' who had collapsed and died while playing five-a-side soccer. 'Toppo', the Lance Todd Trophy winner in the 1979 Challenge Cup Final, had served Trinity for 13 years before enjoying great success with Hull FC, subsequently returning to Wakefield as coach from 1987 to 1994, during which time we won the last-ever Yorkshire Cup Final. Hundreds of mourners, including our present squad, turned out for his funeral at Wakefield Cathedral.

13

DENIED

I had a major shock in the build-up to the 2008 Carnegie Challenge Cup semi-final against Hull FC. The match was scheduled for the Keepmoat Stadium, Doncaster, and it was a game I was looking forward to immensely. I'd played rugby league for over 20 years, from my days as a six-year old with Travellers Saints in Featherstone, and this was to be the biggest fixture in my career to date, even allowing for my appearance the previous year with the Northern Union side against New Zealand.

Then came the hammer blow—one that neither I, nor anyone else other than Wakefield Trinity Wildcats coach John Kear, had expected at all. I was out of the side. And not only out of the side, but out of the squad. Kear had opted for a different line up. I couldn't believe it. It was just another setback in my career and one which, I admit, I found very hard to deal with. I found out the Wednesday before the game. John Kear called me into a one-to-one meeting and he had his reasons, I suppose, but I'd been hoping to write here about the build-up to the match and it didn't happen. It was disappointing to put it mildly. My form had dipped in recent weeks, I can't deny that, but I don't think I was the only one guilty of that. The team as a whole had struggled, possibly because the semi-final had been hanging over our heads. We'd all been looking forward to it and it was probably true to say that our minds had been elsewhere, try as we could to avoid that, in our intervening Super League matches. Obviously I took the bullet for that, as the one to miss out on the big fixture.

The long wait for the semi-final affected me, I don't think there's any getting away from that, but I don't believe it had a bigger impact on my form than on anyone else in the team. It was a massive game for all of us and while it would have been the most important in my career, the same applied I think to most of the other players. Not being included was devastating news, and something I determined to bounce back from. My immediate reaction, so much as I did have one with my mind swirling around, was to get my form back and force my way into the side for the final.

It was difficult and I wasn't the only one in a state of shock. A press conference was arranged for the Thursday, previewing the match, at which most journalists had expected me to be present as a senior player. I didn't attend it as it would have made no sense as I wasn't involved in the match. In fact it could have been an unwelcome diversion for everybody. I'd also taken calls from journalists such as the *Independent*'s Dave Hadfield, wanting to talk to me as a player who, in their opinion, was going to be a key figure in the game. They wanted to interview me as part of the build-up. I suppose that says a lot. Hadfield didn't quite believe me when I told him I'd been dropped, it seemed that he felt it was some kind of trick, or a joke. But it wasn't. I had to be honest with him, and the other reporters, and tell them that I wasn't included; there was no point doing an interview if I wasn't in the team.

I simply couldn't believe I'd been dropped but it was important that I didn't have an adverse affect on the rest of the lads. I didn't want to hang around giving off negative vibes. I needed to be confident in their ability to win the game and it was vital that I help them towards that goal. The situation was a big test of my attitude as a team player and I had to stand up and be counted. John Kear had his reasons for dropping me, and I can't bag him for that. He knew what he was doing and my hope was that he'd made the right decision, and that we'd win. It was important that I stayed positive for the lads. It was hard and I can't deny that my mind was in total turmoil. Any player's career is geared towards matches like that one. Form goes out of the window, as well. Whether you've been playing poorly or well, is irrelevant; you'll lift your game for a semi-final. I'd been looking forward to having a big match and helping take Wakefield Trinity Wildcats to Wembley.

The press had been in touch with me on the basis that my contribution could be vital against Hull. Semi-finals are invariably close affairs and my ability to land drop goals or poach tries had been seen by neutral observers as potentially important. One of my strengths is in picking up tries off little half breaks and it was hard to be denied the chance to contribute in that way in a match of such magnitude. It was a real blow for me, and a real blow for my family. The kids were really looking forward to it, and this was just another setback which, in my distress, led to me wondering whether I'd run over a black cat at some stage in my youth. I phoned Erika in Germany, and she wanted to come home, to support me because she knew how low I'd be feeling. She was as devastated as I was, and all the family shared her upset. It was heartbreaking to be denied the chance to play in a game I'd been building towards all my life.

We had to deal with it, as with other setbacks, and my main hope was that the lads would win and make being dropped a bit easier. It was embarrassing as well as upsetting. Throughout Featherstone people approached me, before the news was released, saying that I must be looking forward to the match. It was hard to turn around and say that I was out. I'm not the first player this kind of thing has happened to of course. Keith Bell, the Featherstone Rovers loose forward, missed out on a Wembley appearance in 1983, coach Alan Agar opting not to select him for a game in which Rovers pulled off a massive upset with a narrow victory over, ironically, Hull. I vaguely know Keith, and it was suggested that I talk to him for an insight into how to deal with such a blow. In such circumstances I tend to turn to my old mentor Tommy Smales who, I have to say, was initially at a loss for words—for the first time ever in my experience—when I told him.

Tommy had seen everything 10 times over during an illustrious playing career which included championship success with Huddersfield and involvement with the reborn Bradford Northern in the mid 1960s, both as captain. He also coached Castleford to Challenge Cup victory in 1970, so he knows what he's talking about. The day of the match was surreal. I watched the game at home on the telly, on my own. It wasn't 'on' for me to go down to the match really, the lads needed to be buzzing. I didn't want them to be distracted by my obvious distress in any shape or form. Some might say I was being selfish by not going but it was vital that I didn't become a negative influence.

In any event, it isn't normal for players outside the squad to be included in match day arrangements. John Kear, for any game, only wants his 19-man squad on the coach, to avoid any distractions from the lads who are not playing. Those players who haven't been included, whether through selection, injury or suspension, can take the option of making their own way and meeting up after the game, which is fair enough. The last thing players want on the bus is people who aren't involved who laugh, joke and carry on. Not that I'd have been laughing and joking. I was down, which was even worse. I wouldn't have wanted that rubbing off on my team-mates.

I wouldn't be human, I suppose, if the episode didn't lead to me considering my future at

Wakefield Trinity Wildcats. I'd been at the club for a long time and I didn't want to do anything drastic. I was fired up about the situation, as any player would be, and it was important that I didn't say anything I would regret later. I was confused by the indication that I would be playing in the Super League fixture with St Helens the following week; I was trying to get my head around that suggestion, when I was considered surplus to requirements for the Hull match. My feeling before the game was that if Wakefield Trinity Wildcats won, John Kear's decision would be vindicated, if they lost, I'd feel even worse because I'd not been out there to try to do anything about it. But he's paid to make those decisions, he knows what he's doing.

He'd opted to play Tevita Leo-Latu, who had not played for eight weeks or so, on the bench, which was another selection the press picked up on. Some also reflected on how Hull would react. I'm seen as a key player—which is why blokes like Dave Hadfield had phoned me for quotes—and it's an old adage in sport that you have to consider how the opposition will react when such a figure is left out. There was a feeling that Hull (and their supporters) would be delighted, one reason being that with me in the side we had three options with field kickers, with our opponents having to monitor Danny Brough, Brad Drew and me. They no longer had to worry about me attempting to clinch the game with a drop goal, and their concerns over the dangers presented by my support play were over. I'd been dreaming of making such contributions for ages, in a game that epitomised the kind of fixture I dearly wanted to play in. My aim had been to come up with a match-winning play; I'd been deprived of a chance to take part in a Challenge Cup semi-final, and I really didn't know where I was going to go from that point.

My confidence was rocked by the news, and I did wonder whether a different challenge was what I needed to reignite the spark in my game. Or I could suddenly score a hat trick the following week against St Helens and be back to my best ... This was definitely the hardest setback of my career to deal with. John was very sympathetic and handled the issue as well as he could. He's done a lot for me and been very helpful and understanding over Brennan, and I'll never blag him off. He told me that it had been a hard decision, but that my form had dipped in recent weeks. That's true, and there was no one else to blame but myself for that, although I'd still say it was true of just about everyone in the squad.

The general malaise was because of the semi-final. I'm not sure why; maybe it's because we're not like St Helens or Leeds, who are in semi-finals and major matches all the time and are therefore able to take them in their stride almost. We're Wakefield Trinity Wildcats and this was the first time the club had been in a semi-final for almost 30 years. It was a big occasion for us, and it's what we, and everyone in the city, had been talking about for the best part of two months. Obviously it had an effect on us, but my disappointment at missing out was at least tempered by Brennan's continued improvement, which helped put the episode in perspective.

Erika was due to return home with Bren and Fletcher the following Thursday for a couple of months. Both were ready to come back and watch a few games at Belle Vue, and Erika was very pleased with how Brennan had progressed. His walking had improved, and by this stage he was doing three laps of a 20-metre room and not wanting to stop. He had really started to enjoy it; when he finished he'd insist, 'Again, again'. His core strength had improved a lot, which was a big help, and this progress would not have happened had we not taken him to Germany. When he first started walking he screamed, possibly because it was hurting him—we don't know for sure—but now he had built up his strength he was starting to really enjoy it. He'd put on weight, his arms were a lot looser and he looked a much healthier child. Almost every day, he was doing something different and improving. He also came out with a different word each day, and they were not even dealing with his speech.

In a year or two's time—when Fletcher is due to start school full time and will have needs of his own—we don't know how much he will have improved, but as parents we are happy that we made that decision. No matter how much the decision to drop me from the team hurt and how big the match was, Brennan's condition was a more important matter for me to worry about; as far as rugby is concerned, one minute you're up, the next you're down. I'm sure I'll still have had more ups in my career than downs when I finally hang up my boots.

As I said earlier, I considered going over to Germany to be with my family after being dropped, but I decided against it. I didn't think I'd be much company for them when the game was on, so my plan was to stick around and watch it on my own, which was a surreal situation. If I'd gone to the game I'd probably have got caught up in the atmosphere and maybe got stripped and run on! I wanted to play so badly. I planned to meet up with the lads afterwards and maybe have a drink, but that had to be the limit of my involvement. Obviously my absence was a key element of the pre-match discussion on TV, with Jonathan Davies and Robbie Paul having their say. John Kear, when he was interviewed on pitch-side only a few minutes before the kick off, indicated that I wasn't so much dropped as he had picked a squad for Hull on a 'horses for courses' basis, which I suppose was fair enough. He didn't go into detail, which of course he wouldn't in the circumstances, even at that late stage shortly before kick off, but one of the pundits may have hit a nail on the head by suggesting that Kear may have wrong-footed Hull, who would probably have spent much of the week working on how to nullify my particular threat.

That could well have been in John's thinking and he was certainly kind enough to refer to my ability, making the point that class is permanent and that there were five weeks to go to the final.

He added that anybody could force their way into the side by then. It turned out to be hypothetical. We lost 32–24 in an amazing game in which we conceded 18 points in the first 10 minutes or so before blasting back to almost rescue the situation. We looked dead and buried in those early stages and to be frank I'm not sure whether my presence would have made any difference. Jamie Thackray—already the subject of controversy, having played for Hull in earlier rounds despite not having been registered for the competition, a fact which many felt should have led to their expulsion—grabbed an early try. The score was allowed after referral to the video referee. Winger Gareth Rayner created a second touchdown by rising high to a kick and palming the ball back, and Graeme Horne added to our problems by racing in. Danny Tickle didn't help matters by converting each score but somehow the lads found their resolve and hit back to within eight points when left winger Matt Petersen squeezed in at the corner off Ryan Atkins' pass, right winger Damien Blanch scoring shortly afterwards with a great collect off Danny Brough's bomb.

Brough goaled one effort and although Hull hit back when Peter Cusak powered over, Tickle again converting, we seemed to go in at the break in the ascendancy after reducing the arrears to 24–20. Brett Ferres sent Tevita Leo-Latu over, Broughie converting, and Hull had a let off when the officials vetoed a penalty shot which went over the top of an upright. We were on top when Atkins raced over seconds before the interval hooter, even if Danny Brough was unable to add the extras.

Unfortunately, Hull had given us too high a mountain to climb. Danny Washbrook extended their lead a minute or two after the restart, Tickle again tagging on the goal. We hit back when Blanch notched his second touchdown but there was a feeling it wasn't going to be our day when Brough's conversion attempt from wide out hit the inside of a post but bounced back. Tickle nosed Hull further ahead with a penalty and our last chance went 10 minutes from time when Blanch, after a lengthy video referral, had what would have been his hat trick try ruled out, the official stating he had been tackled into touch.

So that was it—the Wembley dream was over, with me just a frustrated and helpless onlooker. Who knows if I would have made a difference if I'd been selected? Our bid to reach the Challenge Cup Final was now simply history. It was now a question of focusing on reaching the top six, and the engage Super League play-offs. I also needed to concentrate on helping Brennan develop to the point where he could live life to its fullest, something more manageable and therefore more achievable, than any sporting ambition.

14

DEVASTATING NEWS AND A POSITIVE OUTLOOK

England's performance in the 2008 World Cup was disappointing, there's no getting away from it. I felt for the players and for the coach, Tony Smith, as everyone had expected so much more. I don't doubt that everyone tries their hardest but there's no disputing the fact that, during the tournament as a whole, we fell short. Watching the matches from the other side of the world made me all the more determined to perform well next year and force my way back into the international scene. I'm 28 now, possibly at my peak, and I want to get back to top form in 2009 after what, with hindsight, was a year in which my displays were certainly affected by what was happening at home.

For all that, I've never needed any reminding of the relative unimportance of sport compared to issues in real life. Brennan's treatment and welfare, together with that of our entire family, will always be paramount, as it should be for anyone in any walk of life. Erika and I had some great news as the 2008 season ended when her doctor confirmed that she was pregnant again.

While the pregnancy wasn't planned, we were both overjoyed. It's fantastic for any couple to be told that a child is on the way, and in our case there was added cause for jubilation as we knew that there would be more sibling support for both Brennan and Fletcher in the future. We didn't know what gender the new arrival would be but I suspected that Erika intended to keep going until we produced a girl; I could see us producing an entire rugby league team before she achieved her goal. Brennan continued to show vast improvement, even if there was a long way to go, and it had reached the stage where, when he was in England, he looked forward increasingly to returning to Germany, where he had begun to enjoy his continuing improvement and his developing relationship with Tomasz.

We had a hammer blow when the news came through of Adam Watene's death. I was in Germany at the time, with Erika and the boys, and I thought at first when our prop Danny Sculthorpe phoned me that it was a wind-up. Only nobody, not even the jokers in our squad, would think of a wind-up like that. I couldn't believe it and I still find it hard to credit. Adam keeled over in the gym and never recovered. He had sustained a heart attack and it was beyond belief that he had died. The likeable Cook Islander, who was only 31, was the last person you would think could suffer something like that. He was strong and fit. He didn't smoke, he didn't drink and he was devoted to his family. He was a quiet, dependable bloke, so much so that he was honoured by being chosen as the official consort to the Deputy Lord Mayor of Wakefield, Heather Hudson. That's not the kind of honour bestowed on every sportsman, especially not on someone from the other side of the word, and it says everything about Adam Watene's qualities that he had been called up to the office.

The Mayor, Cllr Jacqui Williams, was obviously very moved when, in announcing a special memorial service at Wakefield Cathedral, she said: 'This is an opportunity for people from across the district to pay their respects to this wonderful person and say their goodbyes. I cannot speak highly enough of Adam and the wonderful way in which he conducted himself in the role of Deputy Mayor's Consort. He will be sadly missed by thousands of people across Wakefield and, indeed, the world including myself, my consort and of course the Deputy Mayor.' This was another instance in which supporters of different clubs have been united in their grief. Only a couple of months after David Topliss' tragic death, when supporters of Wakefield Trinity Wildcats, Hull FC and Oldham banded together as one, Wakefield fans and their equivalents at Castleford Tigers and Bradford Bulls, where Adam had played previously, gathered at Belle Vue to lay wreaths, flowers and offer messages of condolence or to simply stand in stunned disbelief.

His widow, Moana, understandably wished to get his body back to his New Zealand homeland as quickly as she could. Our hearts went out to her. Adam Watene is no longer with us but he certainly won't be forgotten by anyone involved with Wakefield Trinity Wildcats. The tragedy rocked everyone at the club, none more so than coach John Kear, who ripped up his pre-season training schedule. Having focussed his plans, like most other coaches at that time of the year, on the physical side of things, John decided—not surprisingly in the circumstances—to concentrate more on the psychological aspect, opting to rebuild morale after our joint loss. He said, and you couldn't disagree with him: 'Adam's death has knocked us for six, and we will now have to look at our psychological preparations for next season. The last thing I am interested in at the moment is thinking about signing other players. The main priority is to help and support all the people affected by this tragedy.' John was right. Adam Watene's sudden death again put sporting success or failure into its proper perspective, and our defeat in the Carnegie Challenge Cup semi-final and the fact that we had also missed out on making the engage Super League play-offs didn't seem to matter quite as much.

At the same time I think we were all more determined than ever to improve on our performances for the 2009 season, if only as a mark of respect for Adam. We'd not really done ourselves justice in 2008, partly through the diversion of the Challenge Cup semi-final which we allowed to become a debilitating distraction from the League. Our mediocre form in the build-up to the big match with Hull FC at the Keepmoat Stadium, Doncaster, didn't improve much after that demoralising defeat. St Helens came to Belle Vue seven days later, having won their own semi-final against Leeds, determined to build on their status as league leaders. It was a case, though, of 'after the Lord Mayor's show' for them and for us in what was a low-key encounter. I didn't feature in the game but it was as flat watching from the sidelines as it appeared to be on the field of play as the Saints eased to a 42–10 victory without breaking into anything near top gear.

I was back in the side, at last, for the visit of Castleford Tigers the following week and things got no better for the Wildcats, hopes of a top six spot taking a grievous blow with a 48–22 defeat. The general feeling was that I hadn't had a bad game but that was scant consolation for a reverse where we slipped badly after having led by 12 points at one stage. Maybe the only ray of light was that we weren't the only victims of the Tigers in what was a very stage season for them, with the likes of St Helens, Leeds and Warrington (twice) among their victims and Wigan also dropping a point to Terry Matterson's men.

A trip to Wigan wasn't perhaps what we'd have asked for after that humiliating reverse, but the Warriors could have been there for the taking when full back Richie Mathers was sent off in the first half for leading with his elbow against Jason Demetriou. Wigan coach Brian Noble was furious after the match and made it clear that his club would back Richie in any appeal but I think he'd have been even madder if we had won. We didn't. We lost 32–22 in what was another wasted opportunity although John Kear saw plenty of positives in our performance. 'Our attitude was 100 per cent better,' he said. 'We looked, today, as though we wanted to play; we showed desire, commitment and enthusiasm.'

Those qualities, I reckon, were what carried us through an amazing match against Catalans Dragons, when we ended our long losing run with a stunning 38–32 win. It is a game that will live long in the memory of the hundreds of Wildcats fans who made the trip, some of whom could have been forgiven for opting to remain in France had we lost. We blasted into a 22–0 point lead initially but the Dragons roared back impressively to square matters at 32–32. Onlookers said afterwards that our body language sent out all the wrong signals as we trooped back to the centre spot. Maybe (we're not letting on) that was just to lull the opposition into a false sense of security. Danny Brough's kick off couldn't have been better placed and a wicked bounce gave winger Damian Blanch the chance to gain possession which he wasn't inclined to waste. We made the most of the opportunity, using the ball to fine effect for Blanch to grab the winning try. Possibly boosted by that victory, we closed the season with another decent display, although the 30–12 scoreline in a home reverse at the hands of Leeds might not suggest that.

There was a minute's silence in memory of Don Fox, who had passed away a couple of weeks earlier (ironically the Rhinos had provided the opposition for the moment for which he is cruelly best remembered—the missed conversion from the side of the sticks in the 1968 'Watersplash' Final at Wembley). At the break we went in on level terms at 12–12. There was still nothing to separate the sides by the hour mark. I took some satisfaction from a 40/20 but Leeds had the better of the closing quarter, getting into gear for the play-offs and, ultimately, the Super League title— with a 30–12 win. But our performances in our last three games must have persuaded our fans, spinning from what had been a real rollercoaster ride of a season, that we had turned the corner and that we had much to offer for the 2009 campaign.

Brennan, too, was making real progress. As we headed to Christmas 2008 he seemed to be doing something different every week, and there was definitely real light on the horizon. For all that, Erika and I were not expecting miracles and after a number of false dawns during his early treatment we never will. But Brennan's improvement was there for all to see, and it was certainly more noticeable to those who, particularly as he was away for long spells in Germany, didn't get the chance to see him every week. We became used to comments about how much better he looked, and on how he'd progressed, and we knew that people weren't just saying those things to make us feel better.

We hadn't really noticed the improvement ourselves, simply because we were with him every day, and it was a big boost for me to be able to spend some time in Germany at the end of the season with my family. Not that it was all plain sailing. There's something about doors and the Rooneys that doesn't work out, and I became the latest in the family to lock myself out of the apartment while we were over there.

It was while I was alone with Fletcher. He was on the toilet, actually, or to be more precise had finished what he needed to do and was ready to be 'cleaned up'. We'd been waiting for a parcel for a while and just as I was about to start wiping Fletch's bottom I heard the bell ring. The front door was down a longish corridor, with two more doors between. I'm not the slowest bloke around—I hope opposing Super League players will testify to that—but by the time I'd got to the main door the postie had gone, taking our long-awaited parcel with him. I went back to our flat, not best pleased to be blunt, and my mood deteriorated even further when I realised what I'd done. In my rush I'd not propped the door open and it had slammed shut behind me. I'd joined a club which already had Erika and Erika's mum Lynn in membership only it was much worse this time, because our youngest son was locked inside and was on his own. You can imagine my feelings, which were the same as any parent would experience—close to panic.

When I finally got in, it was a sight to see. Fletcher, as was his habit after visiting the toilet, was on his hands and knees—still—patiently (or almost patiently because he wasn't best pleased) waiting to be cleaned up. It could have been worse and I have to admit I was mightily relieved that he was okay. Erika wasn't too happy, as you can imagine, but it was just another little adventure to talk about in future years and something that with hindsight added a bit of light relief to our time in Germany. Brennan was making it all worthwhile. His muscles were certainly nowhere near as tight as they had been, and he had become much more alert. There was a big step forward when he started to feed himself much more efficiently, and everything was without doubt pointing to him having a better life when he eventually reaches adolescence and adulthood.

Most importantly, his progress was gradual and sustainable which, as a professional sportsman, I fully appreciate is the best kind. Most of all, he was enjoying himself while he was in Germany, to the point where he started to cry when he had to come home. Erika and I were also settling a bit more to life in Germany thanks to a couple of friends we made, Jimmy and Hazel. They are from the north east but have a business over there and couldn't do enough to help us. But back in England we had issues to deal with over Brennan's schooling. His school was showing concern about Brennan's education, which was understandable, and we totally understood their point of view, in fact it was also troubling us. But it was a matter of priorities; as his parents, we felt our first duty was to ensure that he could become as physically and mentally able as possible and that meant taking him away from school and to Germany for lengthy periods. The fact that he was improving so much, with his speech getting better all the time, countered the issues over his schooling. Quite simply, we didn't have any real choice.

There was evidence that we were doing the right thing when he continued to walk, with a little help, down the corridor at Tomasz's. Tomasz was tremendous and Brennan always talked about him when we came back home. We were lucky to come across him. It's really not a job for him, they have real concern about the children they have in their care. We've developed a real friendship with them. I suppose that's just as well as Brennan's treatment could continue for another 10, 20 or even 30 years. We simply don't know how long; I suppose it will be until Brennan has made as much progress as he can, when we've reached a point at which nothing more can be done, or until the money runs out.

Our feeling, at Christmas 2008, was that our eldest lad still had a lot of improvement left in him, and we were going to give him every opportunity. Every night when I go to sleep I dream of him walking unaided, and I really do believe that one day Brennan will. I'd swap everything I've achieved in Rugby League for him to do that.

POSTSCRIPT

All sportsmen are used to routine operations, and I'm no different. In fact I've probably had my body tinkered with by the medics more than most. So I had no cause for concern when I made the short trip to Manchester on the eve of the 2009 engage Super League season for a bit of surgery to my knee. I'd been through the same process before, and I knew many other players who had also had their knees cleared out. I'd also had operations on my shoulder in the previous year or two, so as far as I was concerned it was a simple matter of getting onto the operating table, having myself cut open, climbing out of bed and heading home to Featherstone.

Or so I thought, as I went under the anaesthetic.

I had the shock of my life (or should I say, now, of my second life) when I came to surrounded by what seemed to be a host of nurses and doctors. I won't say they were in a panic—that's a condition alien to the medical profession—but there was clearly something amiss. There was more hectic activity going on than I'd expected when I'd slipped away, and there was no hiding the sheer relief on all their faces when I looked, in my haze, around the room and asked what was going on.

That's when I got my shock. I nearly had a heart attack when they told me that my ticker had stopped, for up to half a minute. The surgeon was in a bit of a state over it, as you'd expect. He'd never experienced anything like it before and I was almost tempted to turn the whole situation on its head and offer him a bit of pastoral care. When everything had settled down, it became clear that there was no rhyme or reason to what had happened. The only explanation they could come up with was that because I'm fairly fit (which I should be, as a professional rugby league player) I have a very slow heart rate. That, combined with the anaesthetic, had reduced my pulse to zero. That's my understanding of it, anyway, as a layman.

All I know now that the dust has settled is that I feel very lucky to be alive and that, when I wake up each morning, I thank my lucky stars that I'm still around. Not only for my own sake, either. As a family man, my first thoughts were on how my sons Brennan and Fletcher, not to mention my pregnant wife Erika and our unborn child, would manage without me. I'd lost my own father, of course, and I was a teenager when my dad passed away. That was bad enough but Brennan, at six years old and battling to overcome his cerebral palsy, obviously needs his father around very much. Fletcher, at three years of age, was in a similar position and the idea of me dying shortly before the birth of our third child is not one I wish to dwell upon.

Against that background, I'm simply grateful to be around still and there was some good news for me and my family when I was given the all-clear following a subsequent heart-scan. The assessment, in the cool light of day, is (again, as I understand it) that I'm super-fit and it's because of that that my heart rate slowed to a dangerous level. It's fortunate for me that I was in the right place when it happened, although that's a chicken-and-egg observation, I suppose, given that I was in hospital for an operation anyway.

I feel for John Kear, though. The Wakefield Trinity Wildcats boss is not only a fine rugby league coach, he's a smashing bloke, and we were all still reeling from the death late in 2008, only two or three months earlier, of Adam Watene. John almost started to wonder whether the club was fated in some way, although he's far too rational and level-headed a man to dwell on thoughts such as that for too long. In the end, what happened to me is, by the looks of it, one of those 'one-in-a-million' incidents. There wasn't anything anyone could have done about it and I'm just glad that I was in the right hands when it happened.

In a way, my experience mirrors that of Brennan, whose progress under Tomasz was continuing. The lad was still having it tough, though, and as I was recovering from my scare Brennan was up to his leg-tops in pot, having had an operation on his tendons. His experience, once again, put my own little setback into perspective. They'd had to cut tendons to help put Brennan's hips back into their sockets and to loosen his leg muscles. The big problem is that my eldest son just cannot take painkillers. They simply come right back up again, and the result is that he can take nothing to relive the pain and is in agony. I can't help thinking, in low moments, that we will start to have some good luck one day. And then I reflect that things could be much worse. We've been very lucky to come across Tomasz and Katarzyna at the TheraSuitReha Centre and I was very fortunate to be where I was when my heart stopped.

I don't think I'll be lucky with a request I'm considering putting to John Kear, though. My proposal, if we're all a bit too fit as maybe my experience suggests, is that he lets me off training and that I'm allowed to go on a diet of big breakfasts, including fried bread, followed by fish and chips for lunch and perhaps apple pie and custard for afters. On reflection, perhaps I'll resist putting my idea to him. I've had one escape from near-death; it's best, in all the circumstances I think, not to tempt another.